Living by the Light of the Moon
2014 Moon Book

Beatrex Quntanna

Acknowledgments

I wish to acknowledge…

Jennifer Masters for her ability to capture the essence of the depth and breadth of 2014 with her cover art. She integrated the old wisdom and the new knowledge with such grace, beauty, and style. Thank you, Jennifer! Violet Lyall for her enthusiasm, teamwork, endless nights editing, and keeping me consistent. Michelenne Crab for her tech-support and encouragement for the last 12 years. Michael Makay for the numerological intentions for 365-days, adding a new level of support to our calendar. Kathy Guy for being the *Over-lighting Diva* for the Moon Book.

Special thanks to…

Katherine Sale for the astrological calculations for the entire year. Kaliani Devinne for contributing the Moon charts. Jill Estensen for sharing aspects from her new Astrology system, *Dimensional Astrology*, and adding an innovative approach to experiencing the degrees and the polarity they create for each Moon phase. Last, but not least, a deep gratitude to the countless students who come to Moon Class, without you guys this teaching would not exist.

Book Cover Art

The New Learning Temple by Jennifer Masters
with *Circe Invidiosa* by John William Waterhouse

Book Design & Art Direction

Jennifer Masters
jennifer@new-temple.com

Dimensional Astrology

An innovative translation for the Sabian Symbols
Jill Estensen
intuvision@roadrunner.com

Astrological Calculations

Katherine Sale, MSW, MAc, is an Intuitive Astrologer with a psycho-spiritual approach to counseling, focusing on Soul-Centered Astrology, with an emphasis on the integration of the Soul through the personality.
ksale123@gmail.com

Copyright ©2013 by Beatrex Quntanna
All Rights Reserved. No part of this book may be reproduced or
transmitted in any form or by any means without the written permission
of the publisher, except for the inclusion of brief quotations in a review.

ISBN 978-0-9625292-4-5

Printed in the United States of America

ART ALA CARTE PUBLISHING
760-944-6020
beatrex@cox.net
www. LivingByTheLightOfTheMoon.com
www.beatrex.com

This book is dedicated to
the memory of Nancy Tappe,
my friend, mentor,
master-teacher, and mystic
who inspired the creation
of this book year after year.

Table of Contents

The Importance of Cycles — 6

How to Use This Book — 7

January — 12
New Moon in Capricorn — 14
Full Moon in Cancer — 22
New Moon in Aquarius – Chinese New Year — 30

February — 38
Full Moon in Leo — 40
New Moon in Pisces — 48

March — 56
Full Moon in Virgo — 58
New Moon in Aries — 66

April — 74
Full Moon in Libra – Lunar Eclipse — 76
New Moon in Taurus – Solar Eclipse — 84

May — 92
Full Moon in Scorpio — 94
New Moon in Gemini — 102

June — 110
Full Moon in Sagittarius — 112
New Moon in Cancer — 120

July — 128
Full Moon in Capricorn — 130
New Moon in Leo — 138

August — 146
Full Moon in Aquarius — 148
New Moon in Virgo — 156

September — 164
Full Moon in Pisces — 166
New Moon in Libra — 174

October — 182
Full Moon in Aries – Lunar Eclipse — 184
New Moon in Scorpio – Solar Eclipse — 192

November — 200
Full Moon in Taurus — 202
New Moon in Sagittarius — 210

December — 218
Full Moon in Gemini — 220
New Moon in Capricorn — 228

About the Author — 236
Other Works by This Author — 237

The Importance of Cycles

Each moon cycle offers a different combination of energies. These energies pour down to the Earth, giving us a chance to grow harmoniously into wholeness. The key is to remember that this is a study in light. Following the luminaries, the Sun and the Moon, through the zodiac and noting the cycles of illumination and reflection can bring you to a deeper creative experience of life. The Moon is the great cosmic architect, the builder and dissolver of form and foundation. The Full Moon is about dissolving, and the New Moon is about building. This workbook will assist you in knowing what to build and when, and what to dissolve and when.

The 2014 Moon Book contains a valuable collection of knowledge developed by Beatrex over the years on how to use the moon cycles to enhance the quality of your life. It is a workbook filled with activities to do during each moon cycle, in its specific zodiac sign and time, for the entire year. Life, at the highest spiritual level, moves beyond time and uses cycles to increase your ability to actualize your full potential for living. Cycles are in charge of your personal development; while time is in charge of the change in direction that happens when you take the risk to grow and begin to trust in Divine Timing. This workbook synthesizes techniques that allow for the power of development and direction to occur in the entire spectrum of wholeness. Each zodiac sign holds the knowledge necessary to integrate an aspect of yourself in order to become whole. As the Moon and Sun travel around our planet each month, a different aspect of self-development is presented to you via the constellation (zodiac sign) it is visiting. For centuries, the Moon has been the keeper of the secrets of life. If used appropriately, the Moon sets the stage for successful living. This workbook reveals those secrets and supports you in learning them.

We are now in The Fifth World, a time for co-creation. In order to co-create, we must live in the moment, stay in our truth, accept what is without judgment, and live love. This requires adjustment and a re-calibration down to the core of our beings. It also provides us with newfound freedom that requires us to give up our devotion to our past in order to embark on new frontiers. This year the workbook is set up with a support structure that easily guides you towards awakening your mind in 2014.

When the Moon is Full

When the Moon is full, it is time to set yourself free. The Full Moon is the time when the Moon is in direct opposition to the Sun. This polarity provides a disintegrating effect that presents the best possible opportunity to dissolve anything that stands in the way of your personal freedom. Several hours before a Full Moon you may experience a tension that happens when the Sun and Moon come into an opposing position. This is an aspect that is asking you to learn to understand opposite natures without feeling the need to separate them. As a matter of fact, they are designed to teach you how to find the middle ground and integrate these opposites so that you cannot be manipulated by polarity. Integration creates unity which then creates harmony. The identifying polarity themes are provided for you on the appropriate Full Moon pages. Write down how you would like to be free. Freedom ideas are provided in each Full Moon section of the book to help you make your list.

Once your list is written, light a candle, and read your list out loud. Then, place it under a circle-shaped mirror, and put your candle on top of the mirror. You might put the candle, wishes, and mirror outside in the moonlight or in a special place in your home. Let the candle burn out. For your protection, make sure to use a candle that is in glass, such as a votive or 7-day candle. When your candle has finished burning, your freedom list will be in operation. Remember that being free is as important as co-creating. It is the empty space that makes room for co-creation to occur. Before writing your freedom list you might want to look over the trigger points on the previous page and see if there is anything you might want to let go of before writing your freedom list. Remember to be free is to live without resistance.

Please note: It is best to do your creating and freedom ceremonies at the specific time noted. All times listed in the book are local to the Pacific time zone. Add or subtract hours accordingly to adjust times for your time zone. Visit www.mymoonbook.com for mirrors.

When the Moon is New

When the Moon is new, it is in the same sign as the Sun. This unites the power of the magnetic and dynamic fields that are in perfect resonance for co-creating. This is a potent time to make your desires known to yourself and to the Universe by writing a personal co-creation list. The dates and times are in your workbook, as well as directions and ideas for the development of your co-creation list to actualize. The New Moon page in your book shows the astrological theme to be used in developing your list. While considering the theme provided by the zodiac sign, write your list on the appropriate New Moon page in the workbook. Think about your list like a kid does when writing to Santa Claus. Let yourself become comfortable, while extending the boundaries beyond what you believe is possible. You might consider writing the following words at the end of your co-creation list, "This, or something better than this, comes to me in an easy and pleasurable way for the good of all concerned."

Once your list is written, light a candle, and read your list out loud. Then, place it under an eight-sided mirror, and put your candle on top of the mirror. You might put the candle, wishes, and mirror outside in the moonlight or in a special place in your home. For your protection, make sure to use a candle that is in glass, such as a votive or 7-day candle. Let the candle burn out. By the time the candle burns out, your co-creations are in place and ready to come true.

Please note: It is best to do your creating and freedom ceremonies at the specific time noted. All times listed in the book are local to the Pacific time zone. Add or subtract hours accordingly to adjust times for your time zone. Visit www.mymoonbook.com for mirrors.

How to Use This Book

These Sections Will Help You to Live by the Light of the Moon

Astrological Highlights

This section explains the planets and how they will affect your life each month. It does not contain all of the aspects; it simply highlights points of interest that promote personal growth during each month. If you are interested in more study, take an astrology class. If you are an astrologer and want more information, we have provided a chart for each moon phase for your convenience.

The Monthly Calendar

This section provides you with a monthly overview and keeps you connected to the movements of the Sun, Moon, and planetary cycles. It lets you know when the Moon is void-of-course, when it moves into a new sign, when the Sun and planets change signs, and when a planet goes retrograde or stationary direct (shown by the $\frac{S}{D}$ symbol). As a special treat this year, the calendar has the Tibetan Numerology of the day at the bottom of each square of the grid along with a daily affirmation, written by Michael Makay, to align with the number and set your intentions for the day.

Void Moon

When the Moon is void-of-course, it has made its last major aspect in a sign and stays void until it enters the next sign. When the Moon is void-of-course, you will see the icon V/C on the calendar. This is not a good time to start new projects, relationships, or to take trips, unless you intend to never follow through. When the Moon ☽ enters a new sign, you will see this arrow ➡ It will be followed by the symbol for the new sign and the time that the Moon enters it.

Super-Sensitivity ▲

This happens when the Moon travels across the sky, hits the center of the galaxy, and connects with a fixed star. When this happens the atmosphere becomes chaotic. An extra amount of energy pours down in a spiral at a very fast speed making it difficult to focus. This fragility can make you depressed, anxious, dizzy, and accident-prone. It is a good idea to keep your thought process away from this energy. This is global, not personal.

Low-Vitality ▼

This happens when the Moon is directly opposite the center of the galaxy. When this fixed-star opposition occurs, the Earth becomes very fragile and gets depleted. This leads to exhaustion in our physical bodies and is a sign for us to nurture ourselves by resting. The depletion can create Earth changes. Endings can also happen and resistance to these completions will bring on exhaustion. Best to detach and let go.

The Sun

Each month you will see the icon for the Sun ☉ with an arrow ➡ indicating when the Sun enters a new sign. When the Sun changes signs, the climate of energy takes on a new theme for your personal development. Look for the Sun icon, with an arrow followed by an astrological sign, to indicate sign change and time.

Planets

Planets also change signs and move in retrograde and direct motions. Retrograde planets are next to the date in each day's box followed by retrograde icon ℞. In the middle of each box is information about planetary changes of time and direction.

Please note: All times are given for the Pacific time zone. Add or subtract hours accordingly to adjust times for your time zone.

Choice Points: Motivation – Resistance

These are a part of Dimensional Astrology presenting a prescribed action and resistance for each of the 360-degrees on the astrology wheel. The object of Dimensional Astrology is to depolarize and neutralize motivation and resistance. Each degree for the moon and it's house are described to better enhance your understanding of the phase and its effects on you and your world. For example, in the New Moon in January, the motivation is ambition and the resistance is mediocrity. You will find yourself being driven to be more ambitious. If you resist, you will fall into mediocrity.

Statements

These "I" Statements align the Self with the characteristics of the astrological sign and the house the sign lives in.

Body Mind Spirit

Each astrological sign rules a body part, a mental trait or attitude, and a spiritual condition. This section is provided to increase understanding of the tendencies and patterns that are activated during the moon transit.

Elements

Each Moon Cycle has a primary element (earth, air, fire or water) attached to the constellation it is assigned to and bring you more awareness to work on during the cycle.

House Themes

Each House the moon lands in brings a focus for that moon as a baseline for self-development during the moon phase.

Karmic Awakenings

Every once in a while the chart for the Moon will show an intercepted astrology sign in a house on the chart. This indicates that a karmic pattern is in operation on that day.

Gods and Goddesses

When the Moon enters a new zodiac sign, a changing of guardians occurs. Deep within each sign lives a god or goddess who is the keeper of this cyclical domain. This archetype's assignment is to hold the space for an aspect of wholeness to actualize.

On Your Altar

An altar is an outer focus for inner work. Esoteric coordinates such as tarot cards, flowers, colors, gemstones, fragrance, and numerology are provided as an enhancement to better assist you in working with each moon phase. Perhaps you are working on a love theme; you might want to place six hearts, six flowers, and six gemstones along with your co-creation list and candle. The coordinating tarot card can be used as a visual activation. Flowers, colors, and gemstones accent your intentions. The fragrance provides a special connection to Spirit. You may want to burn candles of this scent, spritz your aura or your altar with the fragrance, or simply sniff the fragrance to awaken your olfactory system. Visit www.mymoonbook.com for moon mists.

List Ideas

Use these ideas to jump start your own lists. Let your imagination take off from here.

Co-Creation List

Write down what you want to create and manifest in your life.

Freedom List

Write down what you want to move beyond in order to set yourself free.

Clearing the Slate for Freedom

This is the first step to freedom and releasing during the Full Moon Cycle. Each section is filled with trigger points that are specific to the astrological sign where the moon resides. See if any of them feel familiar. Acknowledge what's familiar and then follow the instructions by forgiving, releasing, and letting go.

Meditation

This section focuses on the freedom part of the moon cycle.

Challenges and Victories

These are sets of affirmations designed to say out loud during a specific moon cycle to determine a motivational tone for your self-discovery. After saying all of them out loud, you will know which statement applies to you. Circle the one that is yours and use it as a personal mantra daily during the moon phase.

The Astro Wheel

Western astrological charts are placed within a circle or wheel. The wheel is a picture of the sky from a particular place and time on Earth. It is divided into 12 parts called houses. Each house deals with a particular area of life. Key concepts for each house are written outside the wheel. Compare the wheel in the book to your very own chart and discover the theme that you will be living personally during the moon phase.

Cosmic Check-In

"I" statements are designed specifically to keep you in touch with all of the signs and their houses each time the Moon is new or full. Fill in the blanks to complete each statement during each full and new moon phase to activate all parts of your birth chart and keep you in touch with Oneness. Have fun noticing how different you are during each cycle.

Blank Pages

Between each moon phase we have provided blank pages for journaling.

Heavenly Bodies

☉	Sun	Outer personality, potential, director, the most obvious traits of the consciousness projection
☽	Moon	Emotion, feelings, memory, unconsciousness, mother's influence, ancestors, home life
☿	Mercury	The way you think, the intention beneath your thoughts, communication, academia (lower mind)
♀	Venus	Beauty, value, romantic love, sensuality, creativity, social, fun, femininity
♂	Mars	Action, change, variety, sex drive, ambition, warrior, ego, athletics, masculinity
♃	Jupiter	Benevolent, jovial, excessive, expansive, optimistic, abundance, good fortune, extravagant
♄	Saturn	Teacher, karma, disciplined, restrictive, father's influence
♅	Uranus	Liberated, revolutionary, explosive, spontaneous, breakthrough, innovation, technology
♆	Neptune	Mystical, charming, sensitive, addictive, glamor, deceptive, illusions
♇	Pluto	Money, wealth, transformation, secrets, hidden information, sexuality, psychic power
⚷	Chiron	Wounded healer, healing, holistic therapies
☊	North Node	This represents where you are headed in this lifetime. In other words, it represents the direction your life will take you, your future focus. In Eastern astrology, this is sometimes called the "head of the dragon."
☋	South Node	This represents what you brought with you this lifetime and what you are moving away from. It is sometimes called the "tail of the dragon" in Eastern astrology.

Astrological Signs

Each sign of astrology has a particular quality or tone that is described in more detail with the moons.

Sign	"I" Statement		Element	Key Words
♈ Aries	I Am	Sign of the Ram Ruled by Mars ♂ Aries begins the zodiac year with the Spring Equinox	Fire	Ego, identity, championship, leadership, action-oriented, warrior, and self-first.
♉ Taurus	I Have	Sign of the Bull Ruled by Venus ♀	Earth	Self-value, abundant, aesthetic, business, sensuous, art, beauty, flowers, gardens, collector, and shopper.
♊ Gemini	I Communicate	Sign of the Twins Ruled by Mercury ☿	Air	Versatile, expressive, restless, travel-minded, short trips, flirt, gossip, nose for news, and messenger.
♋ Cancer	I Feel	Sign of the Crab Ruled by the Moon ☽ Cancer begins with the Summer Solstice	Water	Emotional, nurturing, family-oriented, home, mother, cooking, security-minded, ancestors, builder of form and foundation.
♌ Leo	I Love	Sign of the Lion and ruled by the Sun ☉	Fire	Willful, dramatic, loyal, children, child-ego state, love affairs, decadent, royal, show-stopper, theatre, adored and adoring.
♍ Virgo	I Heal	Sign of the Virgin Ruled by Mercury ☿	Earth	Gives birth to divinity, perfectionist, discernment, scientific, analytical, habitual, work-oriented, body maintenance, earth connection, attention to detail, service-oriented, earth healer, herbs, and judgmental.
♎ Libra	I Relate	Sign of the Scales Ruled by Venus ♀ Libra begins with the Autumnal Equinox	Air	Relationship, social, harmony, industry, the law, diplomacy, morality, beauty, strategist, logical, and over-active mind.
♏ Scorpio	I Transform	Sign of the Scorpion Ruled by Pluto ♇ and Mars ♂	Water	Intense, passionate, sexual, powerful, focused, controlling, deep, driven, and secretive.
♐ Sagittarius	I Seek	Sign of the Archer Ruled by Jupiter ♃	Fire	Optimistic, generous, preacher-teacher, world traveler, higher knowledge, goal oriented, philosophy, culture, publishing, extravagance, excessive, exaggerator, and good fortune.
♑ Capricorn	I Produce	Sign of the Goat Ruled by Saturn ♄ Capricorn begins at the Winter Solstice	Earth	Ambitious, concretive, responsible, achievement, business, corporate structure, world systems, and useful.
♒ Aquarius	I Know	Sign of the Water Bearer Ruled by Uranus ♅	Air	Inventive, idealistic, utopian, rebellion, innovative, technology, community, friends, synergy, group consciousness, science, magic, trendy, and future-orientation.
♓ Pisces	I Trust	Sign of the Fishes Ruled by Neptune ♆	Water	Sensitive, creative, empathetic, theatre, addiction, escape artist, glamor, secretive, divinely guided, healer, medicine.

The Astrology Wheel

Western astrological charts are placed within a circle or wheel. The wheel is a picture of the sky from a particular place and time on Earth. It is divided into 12 parts called houses. Each house deals with a particular area of life. Below are some key concepts for each house.

	Statement	Ruling Sign		Key Notes
1st House	**I Am**	♈	Aries	Your outer appearance, the way you present yourself, the way you dress, the way you enter a room, and what you leave behind when you leave the room.
2nd House	**I Have**	♉	Taurus	The way you make your money and the way you spend your money.
3rd House	**I Communicate**	♊	Gemini	How you get the word out and the message behind the words.
4th House	**I Feel**	♋	Cancer	The way your early environmental training was and how that set your foundation for living, and why you chose your mother.
5th House	**I Love**	♌	Leo	The way you love and how you want to be loved.
6th House	**I Heal**	♍	Virgo	The way you manage your body and its appearance.
7th House	**I Relate**	♎	Libra	One-on-one relationships, defines your people attraction, and how you work in relationships with the people you attract.
8th House	**I Transform**	♏	Scorpio	How you share money and other resources, what you keep hidden regarding sex, death, real estate, and regeneration.
9th House	**I Seek**	♐	Sagittarius	The way you approach spirituality, philosophy, journeys, higher knowledge, and aspiration.
10th House	**I Produce**	♑	Capricorn	Your approach to status, career, honor, and prestige, why you chose your Father.
11th House	**I Know**	♒	Aquarius	Your approach to friends, social consciousness, team-work, community service, and the future.
12th House	**I Trust**	♓	Pisces	Determines how you deal with your karma, unconscious software, and what you will experience in order to attain mastery by completing your karma. It is also about the way you connect to the Divine.

Tibetan Numerology of the Day

2	**Balance**	Be decisive and move past vacillation.
3	**Fun**	Have a party. Take on a creative project. Express the "Disneyland" side of yourself.
4	**Structure**	Take the day to organize. Get the job done. Work and you will sail through the day.
5	**Action, exercise, travel**	Exercise—join a gym, take a dance class, play tennis, go for a walk. Travel. Go for a drive. Make a change.
6	**Love**	Go out for a night of romance. Work on beauty in your home. Nurture yourself and take care of your health.
7	**Research**	Read a book. Learn something new and get smart. Take a class.
8	**Money**	Have a business meeting. Meet with your accountant. Make a sales call. Start a new business.
9	**Connecting with the Divine**	Meditate. Take part in a humanitarian project. Do community service.
10	**Seeing the big picture**	Take an innovative idea and run with it today!
11	**Completion**	Do what it takes to be complete.

January Planetary Highlights

Venus is Retrograde in Capricorn Until January 31

Venus isn't happy here, she wants love and romance to be the main focus and it's not happening. There will be a feeling of restraint that could lead to a few brat-attacks. Expect to feel limited and entrenched in uninteresting projects.

Jupiter is Retrograde in Cancer for the Entire Month

Expect a rebirth to come forward with some newfound abundance for you. Check in with the idea that other people are interested in presenting you with a treasure chest that has the ability to transform your life.

January 1 – The Sun, Moon, Pluto, and Mercury are All in Capricorn

The Sun, Moon, Pluto, and Mercury are all dancing together in Capricorn asking us to be very clear about what we want to manifest. Whatever we are wishing for right now needs to be fully expressed on four levels: direction (Sun), feelings (Moon), success (Pluto), and communication (Mercury).

January 1-14 – Neptune and Chiron are Coupled in Pisces

Here we look for a healing around avoiding. It is time to rid ourselves of broken promises and face what makes us go into fantasy or addiction instead of facing the music.

January 11 – Mercury Moves into Aquarius

Time to update your computer and related items.

January 14-25 – Jupiter Retrograde Opposite Venus Retrograde

This brings tension between conditional love and unconditional love. There may be some worry that accelerates during this time, based on concern about how lovable you may feel or not feel. Notice how you feel about what you perceive to be the lack of attention from your loved ones and avoid triggering an uncontrollable outrage.

January 19 – The Sun Moves into Aquarius

This is a time when we connect with friends and community to see where a new contribution can be made. Teamwork comes into the foreground and working together can bring about a joyful experience for all concerned.

January 30-February 3 – Venus Retrograde and Pluto are Coupled in Capricorn

This pattern asks for love to go deep on the intimacy level and can result in a profound connection on the Soul level, if used correctly.

January 30 – Neptune in Pisces and Mercury in Aquarius are Coupled

This could become confusing because Neptune gets the smoke and mirrors going to keep the ultra-curious Mercury out of the mystery. Misinterpretation could make things difficult—best to mind your own business.

January 30 – Chinese New Year: Year of the Horse

In Chinese culture, the Horse is a symbol of nobility, class, speed, and perseverance. People born in the Year of the Horse are smart, fabulous speakers who have a gift for getting through to other people. They believe that their aim in life is to seek individual freedom and happiness.

January 31 – Mercury Moves into Pisces

Take time out to meditate with your group and do some self-talk with your own concept of the Divine.

January 31 – Venus goes Direct in Capricorn

Yay, she is released from jail! Head for the light at the end of the tunnel.

Low-Vitality – January 12-13 ▼

This is a time when the Earth is in a low energy pocket; there is not enough vitality available to go into a charged surge. Do what it takes to go with the flow and rest, instead of pushing the envelope. Resistance wears you down.

Super-Sensitivity – January 26-27 ▲

During this time the global atmosphere is very sensitive. Avoid travel, if possible, and stay in places that promote your relaxation. Negative thinking can be a part of this pattern; don't become your mind. Spiraling thoughts can take you into a depression if you buy into the global atmosphere.

♈ Aries	♋ Cancer	♐ Sagittarius	☽ Moon	♄ Saturn	☊ North Node	V/C Void-of-Course
♉ Taurus	♌ Leo	♑ Capricorn	☿ Mercury	♅ Uranus	☋ South Node	▲ Super-Sensitivity
♊ Gemini	♍ Virgo	♒ Aquarius	♀ Venus	♆ Neptune	➡ Enters	▼ Low-Vitality
	♎ Libra	♓ Pisces	♂ Mars	♇ Pluto	℞ Retrograde	
	♏ Scorpio	☉ Sun	♃ Jupiter	⚷ Chiron	S/D Stationary Direct	

My Co-Creation List

Capricorn
Co-Creation Ideas

Now is the time to focus on manifesting flexibility, productivity, authenticity, timing, new paradigms, transmuting, transformation, and re-translating structure.

This, or something better than this, comes to me in an easy and pleasurable way for the good of all concerned. Thank you, Universe!

New Moon in Capricorn

January 1, 3:14 AM

Capricorn Challenges and Victories

Say all of the statements in this section out loud. Then, underline the phrase that means the most to you. Use the phrase as your special affirmation for manifesting and co-creating throughout this phase of the moon.

Ultimate fulfillment is mine today! My willingness to live my life to the fullest, each day, is making all of my dreams come true. I am fulfilling the promise of my destiny, and, in so doing, I make my mark on the world. I have completed my commitment to the Earth and to the cosmos by being all that I can be in the cycles of time on the inner and outer planes of awareness. All four seasons have been activated within me, so that I am in alignment and in motion with the cycles of releasing, rebirthing, planting, and harvesting. I can now claim my citizenship in all four worlds. I am open and ready for the inspiration that the spirit world brings me. I am ready to conquer the mental world by using thought, rather than thinking. I am open to the expression of my heart and the magnetic field of love that is ever-present in my experience. I am open to receive abundance from Nature and I contribute to the physical world by actively manifesting my ideas into reality. I am in harmony with the four elements and keep them active within me, as well as contribute to them externally. The element of air is within me as I breathe in the miracle of life. The element of earth is within me as I honor my body and use all of its senses to enhance the quality of life. I honor the Earth as my home and take complete stewardship of my home and property on this Earth. I honor the water, the wellspring of life eternal, and allow for the flow of my feelings and emotions to be a creative influence on the unconscious and conscious planes. I honor the fire within me as the spark of light that is a source of inspiration in my experience, and, in so doing, I have fulfilled the promise of my destiny to live fully, freely, and passionately on all levels and on all dimensions with my Earth-Cosmos connection.

Capricorn Homework

The Capricorn Moon is the reincarnation of Spirit, emerging from the dark waters of our past emotions and releasing us from our fears of change and loss. Awaken your powerful and positive spiritual connection to be open to new possibilities. Ask yourself to move beyond your emotional loyalty to the past in order to co-create. We are reminded of our need for material and emotional security at this time. In order to insure this, we must learn to build a foundation for ourselves that is lit from within, and made from the materials of love, goodwill, and intelligence. Give yourself permission to throw away your watch and celebrate living in the moment.

Without Acknowledgment Progress Cannot Occur

Acknowledgment creates space for victory and gratitude, which automatically brings us to a level of completion so a new cycle of opportunity can occur in our lives. When we celebrate our wins and acknowledge our victories with gratitude, we update our cells so that our ability to move forward is not hindered by a cellular holographic pattern that is stuck in the past. Cellular lag creates resistance and makes moving forward most difficult. The key is to stay continuously updated by acknowledging yourself for what you did do at the end of each day rather than heading off to sleep thinking about what you did not do. By acknowledging what we didn't do, we play into our karmic storage bank and keep our progress at bay. When we acknowledge ourselves and our manifestations, we are complete, and more cycles of opportunity become available to us in each new day. Be prepared for miracles.

Victory List

Gratitude List

This fulfills the relationship between the giver and the receiver, which completes the cycle with the Universe so that a new beginning can be established.

New Moon in Capricorn

January 1, 3:14 AM

How to Use the Moon Book With Your Chart

Fill in the blanks on the Cosmic Check-In page. Then look up the degree of the moon on the chart below. Take note of the "I" statement on the outside of the wheel where the moon is located. Now locate the same degree on your own chart, and make a note of the house and corresponding "I" statement. Go back to the Cosmic Check-In page and circle the two statements from the charts and read what you wrote. This will give you an idea about what to expect from this moon phase on a personal level.

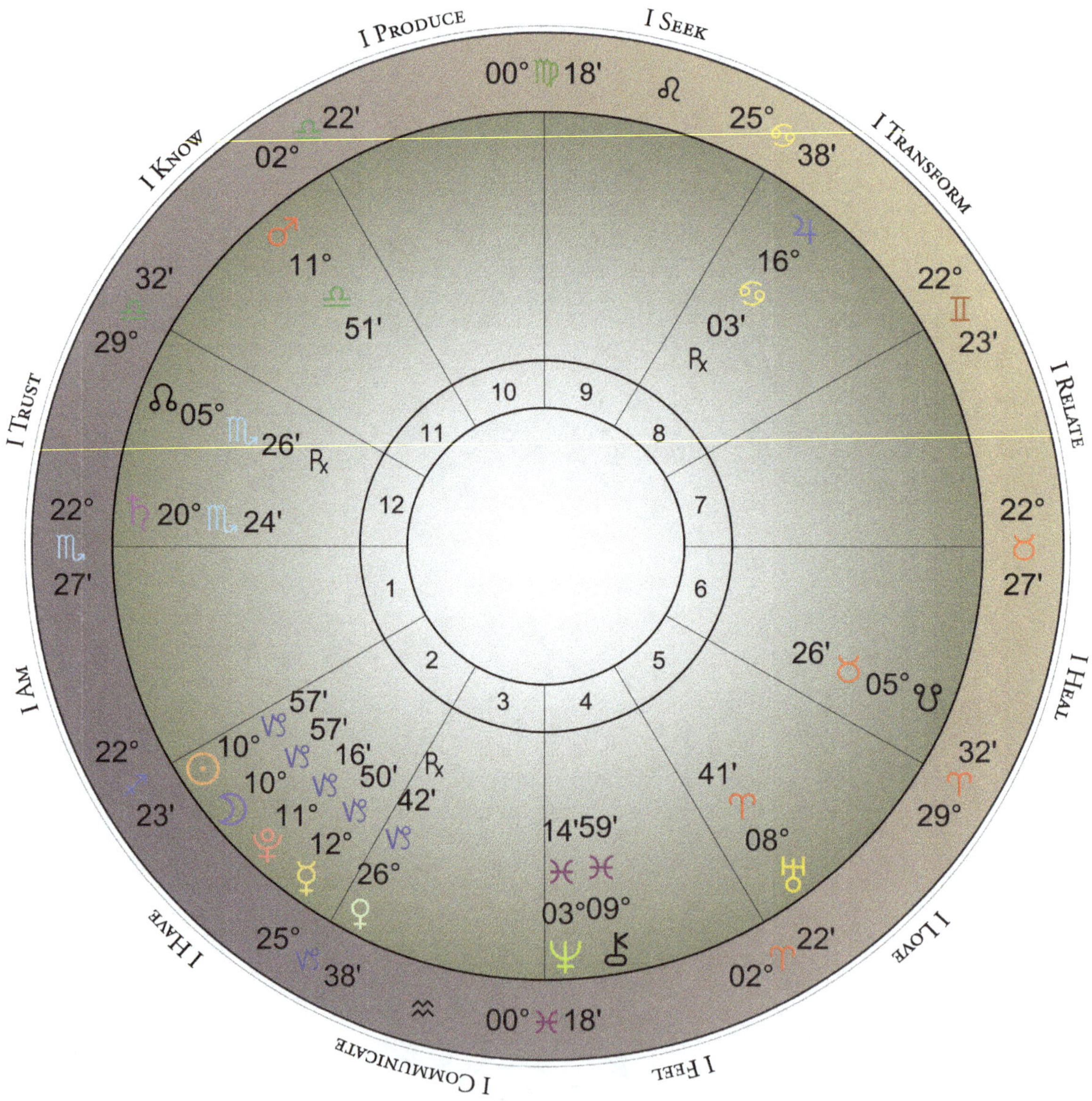

♈ Aries	♋ Cancer	♐ Sagittarius	☽ Moon	♄ Saturn	☊ North Node	V/C Void-of-Course
♉ Taurus	♌ Leo	♑ Capricorn	☿ Mercury	♅ Uranus	☋ South Node	▲ Super-Sensitivity
♊ Gemini	♍ Virgo	♒ Aquarius	♀ Venus	♆ Neptune	➡ Enters	▼ Low-Vitality
	♎ Libra	♓ Pisces	♂ Mars	♇ Pluto	℞ Retrograde	
	♏ Scorpio	☉ Sun	♃ Jupiter	⚷ Chiron	S/D Stationary Direct	

Cosmic Check-In

Take a moment to write a brief phrase for each "I" statement.
This activates all areas of your life for this creative cycle.

♑ I Produce

♒ I Know

♓ I Trust

♈ I Am

♉ I Have

♊ I Communicate

♋ I Feel

♌ I Love

♍ I Heal

♎ I Relate

♏ I Transform

♐ I Seek

Full Moon in Cancer

January 15, 8:52 PM

The Sun is Opposite the Moon

Full Moons are always in opposition to the Sun. This creates a feeling of tension between where you want to shine and how your feelings are flowing on a sensory level about the Sun's directive. The two forces seem like they are working against each other, yet they are on the same team displaying different techniques to attain the same mission. The Cancer/Capricorn polarity creates tension about being at home with family or being at work positioning yourself for success.

Cancer Goddess

Demeter is the goddess of Nature's abundance. When her family was disrupted and her child taken, Demeter withheld nourishment from the Earth, and Nature stopped producing. The people weren't nourished and withheld their honoring of the gods. As a result, an agreement was struck between Heaven and Earth. Demeter agreed to let go, and release full control of her child, and restore Nature's abundance in exchange for a new, balanced relationship with her daughter. When the Moon is Full in Cancer, it is time to look at our mother/child issues and release what is no longer nurturing to us.

On Your Altar

Colors Shades of gray and milky, creamy colors

Numerology 5 – variety, power, and expansion

Tarot Card The Chariot – the ability to move forward

Gemstones Pearl, moonstone, ruby

Plant remedy Shooting Star – the ability to move straight ahead

Fragrance Peppermint – the essence of the Great Mother

Degree Choice Points
25° Cancer 58'

Motivation Informed reflection

Resistance Complacency

Statement I Feel
Body Stomach
Mind Worry
Spirit Nurturing

Element
Water – Motion without resistance, the gateway to all things hidden, conscious and unconscious.

Eleventh House Moon
15° Cancer 16'

Motivation Interpretation

Resistance Scheming

Eleventh House Umbrella Theme
I Know – Your approach to friends, social consciousness, teamwork, community service, and the future.

Meditation

The freedom themes are provided by the zodiac sign and can be from this lifetime or other lifetimes. These meditations assist in dissolving blocks and opening pathways to new frontiers.

When the Moon is in Cancer, it is time to reconcile with past events. Sit quietly and breathe, in and out, until you are settled. Ask for an angel of records to show you a time when your need was not fulfilled. It is important to listen to our emotional nature and take time out to be nurtured. Reflection and illumination are the main themes while sinking deeply into the subconscious memory. During the Cancer Moon, it is time to research your Soul's records to release past memories of wrongs enacted against you so you can move beyond any attachment to self-pity.

Cancer Challenges and Victories

Say all of the statements in this section out loud. Then, underline the phrase that means the most to you. Use the phrase as your special affirmation for manifesting and co-creating throughout this phase of the moon.

Today, I take advantage of my ability to take action and position myself for success. I clearly know that the road to success is before me, and all I need to do is move forward. I am aware that when I take action and move forward, the Universe fills in the dots. Whether I move left, right, or straight ahead doesn't matter—what matters is that I am in movement. Today, I release indecisiveness that keeps me stuck. Today, I let go of vacillation that exhausts my mind. Today, I take my foot off of the brakes and find the gas pedal. I allow movement to occur, even if I don't know where I am going. When I take action, I trust the guideposts will appear. I am aware that action leads me to my new direction. Today, I know and GO! I remember that Karma comes to the space of non-action, while success comes through action. Action brings me to my victory. Standing still leads to regret, resentment, and chaos. I am aware that action can be as simple as taking a walk on the beach, buying fresh flowers to add a new dimension to my home, or simply going to a new restaurant for lunch. I take action today to break up a crystallized pattern and, in so doing, my life begins to show me newfound awareness and light to guide me.

Cancer Homework

It's now time to conquer pride and ambition, overcome fear of loneliness, release the need for money, security, and possessions, discover the value of emotions, and connect to beauty. Submerge yourself in a tub of water, relax, and let the clean water flow through your cells to wash away all of your hurts, resentments, and history that keep you trapped in the past. Pull the plug and let the spiral of water carry away your pain. Be prepared to boldly claim your presence in the present. Look around your kitchen and throw away the pots and pans that continue to feed your past, rather than vitalizing your life now.

Full Moon in Cancer

January 15, 8:52 PM

Clearing the Slate for Freedom

Remember a time when you experienced the following trigger points. Write down what happened, forgive yourself, release it, and let it go to clear your slate for freedom.

Blame

- Forgive
- Release
- Let go

Attachment to Things

- Forgive
- Release
- Let go

Emotional Attachment to the Past

- Forgive
- Release
- Let go

Self-pity

- Forgive
- Release
- Let go

Broken Promises

- Forgive
- Release
- Let go

My Freedom List

Cancer Freedom List Ideas

Now is the time to set myself free from self-pity, defensive behavior, nurturing everyone else but me, living in the past, being a mother, and having a mother.

Full Moon in Cancer

January 15, 8:52 PM

How to Use the Moon Book With Your Chart

Fill in the blanks on the Cosmic Check-In page. Then look up the degree of the moon on the chart below. Take note of the "I" statement on the outside of the wheel where the moon is located. Now locate the same degree on your own chart, and make a note of the house and corresponding "I" statement. Go back to the Cosmic Check-In page and circle the two statements from the charts and read what you wrote. This will give you an idea about what to expect from this moon phase on a personal level.

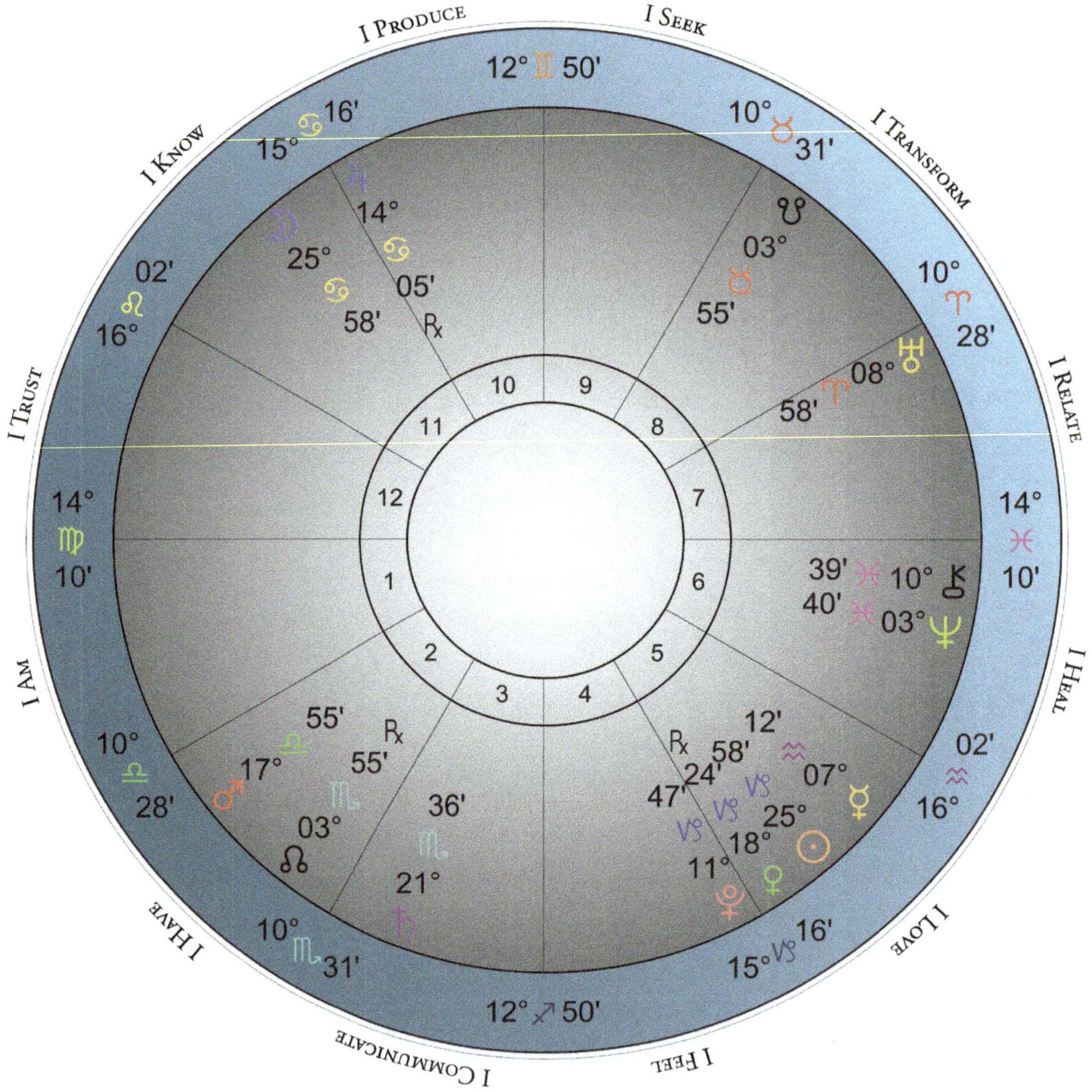

♈ Aries	♋ Cancer	♐ Sagittarius	☽ Moon	♄ Saturn	☊ North Node	V/C Void-of-Course
♉ Taurus	♌ Leo	♑ Capricorn	☿ Mercury	♅ Uranus	☋ South Node	▲ Super-Sensitivity
♊ Gemini	♍ Virgo	♒ Aquarius	♀ Venus	♆ Neptune	➡ Enters	▼ Low-Vitality
	♎ Libra	♓ Pisces	♂ Mars	♇ Pluto	℞ Retrograde	
	♏ Scorpio	☉ Sun	♃ Jupiter	⚷ Chiron	S/D Stationary Direct	

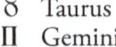

Cosmic Check-In

Take a moment to write a brief phrase for each "I" statement.
This activates all areas of your life for this creative cycle.

♋ I Feel

♌ I Love

♍ I Heal

♎ I Relate

♏ I Transform

♐ I Seek

♑ I Produce

♒ I Know

♓ I Trust

♈ I Am

♉ I Have

♊ I Communicate

New Moon in Aquarius

January 30, 1:38 PM – Chinese New Year

Degree Choice Points
   10° Aquarius 55'

Motivation Applied inspiration

Resistance Self-absorption

Statement I Know
   Body Ankles
   Mind True genius
   Spirit Vision

Element
   Air – Inspiration; the breath of life allows the mind to achieve new insights and fresh perspectives.

Ninth House Moon
   8° Aquarius 58'

Motivation Accomplishment

Resistance Pretension

Ninth House Umbrella Theme
   I Seek – The way you approach spirituality, philosophy, journeys, higher knowledge, and aspiration.

Chinese New Year – Enter the Horse

In Chinese culture, the Horse is a symbol of nobility, class, speed and perseverance. People born in the Year of the Horse are smart, fabulous speakers who have a gift for getting through to other people. They believe that their aim in life is "to seek individual freedom and happiness."

When the Sun is in Aquarius

This is a time when the higher octave of the mind comes into play and one is given the power of vision. The Aquarian energies promote knowing by being a wellspring of knowledge. They expand the radius of contact by going beyond the known in areas of communication and cooperation. Now is the time to be initiated into greater awareness to serve the fields of human endeavors. Connect and combine magic with science and become a creative influence. When the sun is in Aquarius we transform thinking into knowing, which is the key to living a successful life in 2014.

Aquarius Goddess

The Aquarian goddess, Star Woman, is also known as Hathor, the keeper of the light who gives birth to insight. All goddesses are born from the stars. Star Woman is in charge of directing the light bodies through the void of Creation to the point of insight, which occurs when the radiance is instilled in the memory of creation. She instills the light of the world into your own being so you can become in service to the souls who have lost their way.

On Your Altar

Colors Violet, neon, crystalline rainbow tints

Numerology 11 – meditation adds energy to your life

Tarot Card The Star – golden opportunities for the future

Gemstones Aquamarine, blue topaz, peacock pearls

Plant Remedy Queen of the Night cactus – ability to see light in the dark

Fragrance Myrrh – heals the nervous system

My Co-Creation List

Aquarius
Co-Creation Ideas

Now is the time to focus on manifesting vision, invention, technology, freedom, friends, community, personal genius, higher awareness, teamwork, science, and magic.

This, or something better than this, comes to me in an easy and pleasurable way for the good of all concerned. Thank you, Universe!

New Moon in Aquarius

January 30, 1:38 PM – Chinese New Year

Aquarius Challenges and Victories

Say all of the statements in this section out loud. Then, underline the phrase that means the most to you. Use the phrase as your special affirmation for manifesting and co-creating throughout this phase of the moon.

Today, I chart my course for my new direction. My future is set on a new, fresh evolutionary course. I am guided by a higher source and trust in that guidance. I know my life has value and I am willing to contribute to the pool of consciousness by experiencing my life and living my life to the fullest view of possibility. Today, I know my possibilities are endless. My Spirit and my Soul are connected to Heaven and to Earth and this knowing brings me to the awareness that I can add to the higher qualities of life because I am connected to the whole. My being is far reaching and immeasurable. I contribute to existence simply by knowing. All of the guideposts are connected for me today to see my way to a profound new future. My vision is clear and I can clearly set my sights on this new course. Golden opportunities come with this new vision and I trust in my guidance to bring me to this new level of manifesting power. I check in with my inner lights, each day, by meditating and asking for all seven of the energy centers in my body to come into alignment with the outer symbols of guidance. I do this by becoming still and breathing until I feel the stillness. Then, I place my hand on each center in my body, one center at a time, to be activated by light. Next, I ask out loud for each center in my body to let me know what its energetic contribution to the new direction is and how best to use the energy to move forward on my new course of action. I write down each statement and connect each statement to the guiding star in the sky. I am now linked up physically and spiritually and ready to navigate my total self towards my new evolutionary direction.

Aquarius Homework

Aquarians co-create a storehouse of information through innovative telecommunications, technology, social networking and media, and global communication. They are typically found in the fields of psychology, science fiction authoring or film-making, speech writing, and aerospace engineering.

Consider these three Aquarian gifts:

- Opportunity – become a creative influence
- Enlightenment – when you become aware that you are light
- Brotherhood – separation doesn't exist anymore

Where do you see these occurring in your life?

Without Acknowledgment Progress Cannot Occur

Acknowledgment creates space for victory and gratitude, which automatically brings us to a level of completion so a new cycle of opportunity can occur in our lives. When we celebrate our wins and acknowledge our victories with gratitude, we update our cells so that our ability to move forward is not hindered by a cellular holographic pattern that is stuck in the past. Cellular lag creates resistance and makes moving forward most difficult. The key is to stay continuously updated by acknowledging yourself for what you did do at the end of each day rather than heading off to sleep thinking about what you did not do. By acknowledging what we didn't do, we play into our karmic storage bank and keep our progress at bay. When we acknowledge ourselves and our manifestations, we are complete, and more cycles of opportunity become available to us in each new day. Be prepared for miracles.

Victory List

Gratitude List

This fulfills the relationship between the giver and the receiver, which completes the cycle with the Universe so that a new beginning can be established.

New Moon in Aquarius

January 30, 1:38 PM – Chinese New Year

How to Use the Moon Book With Your Chart

Fill in the blanks on the Cosmic Check-In page. Then look up the degree of the moon on the chart below. Take note of the "I" statement on the outside of the wheel where the moon is located. Now locate the same degree on your own chart, and make a note of the house and corresponding "I" statement. Go back to the Cosmic Check-In page and circle the two statements from the charts and read what you wrote. This will give you an idea about what to expect from this moon phase on a personal level.

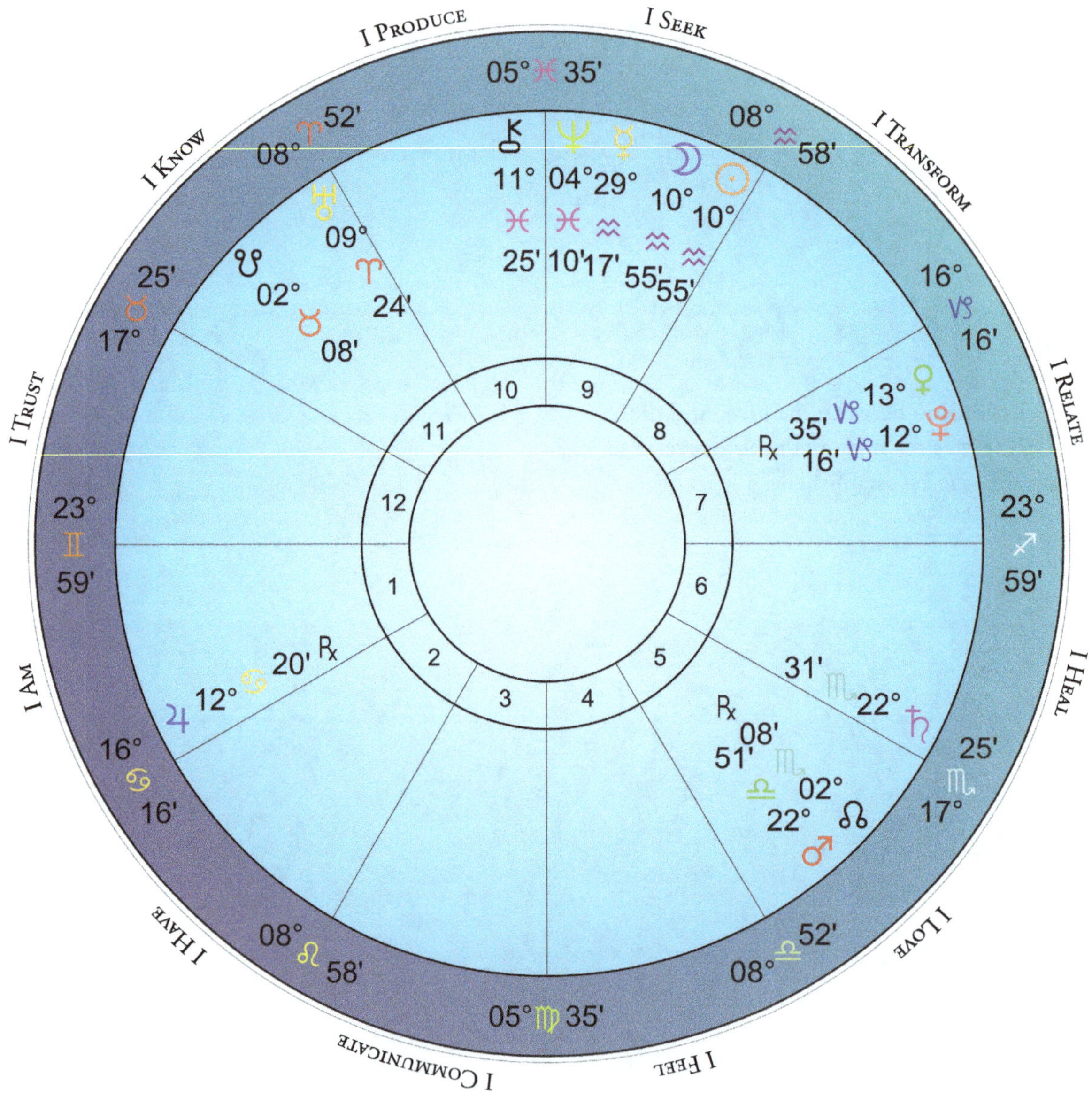

♈ Aries	♋ Cancer	♐ Sagittarius	☽ Moon	♄ Saturn	☊ North Node	V/C Void-of-Course
♉ Taurus	♌ Leo	♑ Capricorn	☿ Mercury	♅ Uranus	☋ South Node	▲ Super-Sensitivity
♊ Gemini	♍ Virgo	♒ Aquarius	♀ Venus	♆ Neptune	➡ Enters	▼ Low-Vitality
	♎ Libra	♓ Pisces	♂ Mars	♇ Pluto	℞ Retrograde	
	♏ Scorpio	☉ Sun	♃ Jupiter	⚷ Chiron	S/D Stationary Direct	

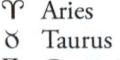

Cosmic Check-In

Take a moment to write a brief phrase for each "I" statement.
This activates all areas of your life for this creative cycle.

♒ I Know

♓ I Trust

♈ I Am

♉ I Have

♊ I Communicate

♋ I Feel

♌ I Love

♍ I Heal

♎ I Relate

♏ I Transform

♐ I Seek

♑ I Produce

February Planetary Highlights

Jupiter Retrograde in Cancer for the Entire Month

This is a good time to get a health check-up and tend to your body by making new healthy choices. The concept of vitality comes into play here in your body.

February 6 – Mercury goes Retrograde in Pisces

Expect a steam cleaning of your emotions. Take into consideration that Mercury has a tendency to just scrape the surface of feelings while simply chattering away about what comes up. On the other side of the coin, Pisces wants to go deep into the flow and connect the dots with the Divine to get answers.

February 12 – Mercury Retrograde Moves into Aquarius

This brings on the crisis for the year of "learning the difference between thinking and knowing." It is time for our minds to recalibrate how we think and move into knowing.

February 14 – The Sun and Mercury Retrograde in Aquarius Opposing the Moon in Leo

The idea of feeling free and being adored could create some tension and questioning from the mind. Allow the power of the Sun to direct you to your answer and all will be well.

February 14 – Venus Coupled with Pluto in Capricorn

Venus is not happy in "stick-in-the-mud" Capricornville because she is asked to be responsible and practical. Meeting up with sexy Pluto adds a new dimension to her visit here. Get ready for an integration to happen between sex and sensuality, where deep intimacy replaces frivolous flirting. Dive deep!

February 18 – North Node Moves into Libra

A major game changer happens here regarding relationship. The archetype for marriage and partnership is now ready for renewal after being stuck in survival mode for the last 100 years. This will activate a very deep connection to the idea of honesty and integrity never before felt in the area of relating. The "old guard" idea of needing to prove yourself drops off the grid and makes space for a true partnership to actualize.

February 18 – The Sun Moves into Pisces

Expect something out of the blue to come forth to be dealt with on a conscious level. It may have a familiar feeling in your gut as it arrives, as if you have been waiting for this moment for your entire life. Now is the time for Mastery. Remember that the Universe doesn't give you anything that you can't handle.

February 28 – Mercury goes Direct in Aquarius

Get ready for a major dose of innovation to burst forward and advance your life to a new level. Rocket fuel will advance you forward to a new realm of magic, moving beyond the known.

February 28 – Mars and North Node Conjunct in Libra

The dynamic components of relating will be fused with a new current to explore as the new partnership archetype actualizes. Expect a new kind of action to be born and notice your attraction force expand.

February 28 – Neptune, Moon, Sun, and Chiron Conjunct in Pisces

Expect to be fueled by some idealistic dream keeping you seduced by your emotional loyalty to your past. Do whatever you can to shed the sunlight of reality on this, so you can be healed instead of seduced and stuck.

Low-Vitality – February 8-9 ▼

This is a time when the Earth is in a low energy pocket; there is not enough vitality available to go into a charged surge. Do what it takes to go with the flow and rest instead of pushing the envelope. Resistance wears you down. Earth changes are possible at this time.

Super-Sensitivity – February 23-24 ▲

This is a time when the global atmosphere is very sensitive. Avoid travel, if possible, and stay in places that promote your relaxation. Negative thinking can be part of this pattern; don't become your mind. Spiraling thoughts can take you into a depression if you buy into the global atmosphere.

♈ Aries	♋ Cancer	♐ Sagittarius	☽ Moon	♄ Saturn	☊ North Node	V/C Void-of-Course
♉ Taurus	♌ Leo	♑ Capricorn	☿ Mercury	♅ Uranus	☋ South Node	▲ Super-Sensitivity
♊ Gemini	♍ Virgo	♒ Aquarius	♀ Venus	♆ Neptune	➡ Enters	▼ Low-Vitality
	♎ Libra	♓ Pisces	♂ Mars	♇ Pluto	℞ Retrograde	
	♏ Scorpio	☉ Sun	♃ Jupiter	⚷ Chiron	S/D Stationary Direct	

February

SUNDAY	MONDAY	TUESDAY	WEDNESDAY	THURSDAY	FRIDAY	SATURDAY
						1 ♃ᴿ 4. Friendship is a foundation for love.
2 ♃ᴿ Groundhog Day ☽ V/C 8:34ᴀᴍ ☽→♈ 8:54ᴘᴍ 5. Put more variety in your life.	**3** ♃ᴿ 6. Enjoy your people skills.	**4** ♃ᴿ ☽ V/C 3:14ᴘᴍ 7. Learn something new from a friend.	**5** ♃ᴿ ☽→♉ 1:46ᴀᴍ 8. Give from a generous heart.	**6** ☿♃ᴿ ☿ᴿ-3°♓19' 1:44ᴘᴍ ☽ V/C 8:49ᴘᴍ 9. Pray out loud for what you desire.	**7** ☿♃ᴿ ☽→♊ 10:43ᴀᴍ 10. Look forward to a new day.	**8** ☿♃ᴿ ▼ 11. Count your many blessings.
9 ☿♃ᴿ ▼ ☽ V/C 9:04ᴘᴍ ☽→♋ 10:32ᴘᴍ 3. Know that you are creative.	**10** ☿♃ᴿ 4. Balance creates a good foundation.	**11** ☿♃ᴿ 5. Remember exercise is essential.	**12** ☿♃ᴿ ☿ᴿ→♒ 7:31ᴘᴍ ☽ V/C 2:51ᴀᴍ ☽→♌ 11:15ᴀᴍ 6. Be responsible for what you cause.	**13** ☿♃ᴿ 7. Do not overthink the situation.	**14** ☿♃ᴿ Valentine's Day ○26°♌13' 3:53 ᴘᴍ ☽ V/C 7:13ᴘᴍ ☽→♍ 11:25ᴘᴍ 8. Lead by example.	**15** ☿♃ᴿ 9. Let your spirit soar.
16 ☿♃ᴿ ☽ V/C 9:04ᴘᴍ 10. See each day as a new beginning.	**17** ☿♃ᴿ President's Day ☽→♎ 10:22ᴀᴍ 2. Once you decide, then act.	**18** ☿♃ᴿ ☊→♎ 8:22ᴀᴍ ☉→♓ 10:01ᴀᴍ 3. Laughter can be the best medicine.	**19** ☿♃ᴿ ☽ V/C 1:52ᴘᴍ ☽→♏ 7:32ᴘᴍ 4. Create the structure that works.	**20** ☿♃ᴿ 5. Enjoy solitude and activity.	**21** ☿♃ᴿ ☽ V/C 2:09ᴘᴍ 6. Stand by a friend in need.	**22** ☿♃ᴿ ☽→♐ 2:11ᴀᴍ 7. Awaken the wisdom within.
23 ☿♃ᴿ ▲ 8. Show respect for all people.	**24** ☿♃ᴿ ▲ ☽ V/C 1:25ᴀᴍ ☽→♑ 5:50ᴀᴍ 9. Donate to a humane cause.	**25** ☿♃ᴿ 10. Breathe deeply and move on.	**26** ☿♃ᴿ ☽ V/C 2:51ᴀᴍ ☽→♒ 6:55ᴀᴍ 11. See potential everywhere.	**27** ☿♃ᴿ 3. Put more play into your life.	**28** ♃ᴿ ●10°♓39' 11:59ᴘᴍ ☿ᴅ-18°♒9' 6:01ᴀᴍ ☽ V/C 2:54ᴀᴍ ☽→♓ 6:52ᴀᴍ 4. Don't overwork the situation.	

Full Moon in Leo

February 14, 3:53 PM

Degree Choice Points
26° Leo 12'

Motivation Quickening

Resistance Illusion

Statement I Love
  Body Heart
  Mind Self-confidence
  Spirit Generosity

Element
Fire – passion, enthusiasm, being centered in personal identity, ability to direct will.

First House Moon
6° Leo 12'

Motivation Seeing the "big picture"

Resistance Starstruck

First House Umbrella Theme
I Am – Your outer appearance, the way you present yourself, the way you dress, the way you enter a room, and what you leave behind when you leave the room.

Karmic Awakening

Childhood issues dealing with collecting what is valued and letting go of what no longer has value.

The Sun is Opposite the Moon

Full Moons are always in opposition to the Sun. This creates a feeling of tension between where you want to shine and how your feelings are flowing on a sensory level about the Sun's directive. The two forces seem like they are working against each other, yet they are on the same team displaying different techniques to attain the same mission. The Leo/Aquarius polarity creates tension about the need to be adored and the need to be free.

Leo God

Apollo, the god of light, is gifted with extraordinary beauty and insight. Despite his magnificent beauty, he never experienced the true heart-connection in love. He took the name of the Sun god; however, he has never performed his duties as such. He is personified as the ideal male, standing for order and reason. The gateway of his temple is inscribed with a statement, "Know Thyself." He attracted many adoring people because of his beauty, yet they never entered the realm of his heart. During the Full Moon in Leo, we must set ourselves free from the facets of emptiness that come from the desire to be adored rather than to be loved and loving.

On Your Altar

Colors Royal purple, gold, orange

Numerology 8 – lead by example

Tarot Card Strength – passion for all of life

Gemstones Amber, emerald, pyrite, citrine, yellow topaz

Plant remedy Sunflower – standing tall in the center of life

Fragrance Jasmine – remembering your Soul's original intention

Meditation

The freedom themes are provided by the zodiac sign and can be from this lifetime or other lifetimes. These meditations assist in dissolving blocks and opening pathways to new frontiers.

When the Moon is in Leo, we have the opportunity to see the records of our Soul's original intent. Close your eyes and take in a few deep breaths. Then, ask to make contact with an Angel of Records. Once that has been established, ask to be shown a time when you lost your original intent and replaced it with self-appointed authority. Honesty is the key to the Leo Moon. Ask for help to set yourself free from the self-appointed authority and accept the grace that reconnects you to your original intention. The Leo Full Moon connects solar power to your power, and the angel brings a refreshment of grace.

Leo Challenges and Victories

Say all of the statements in this section out loud. Then, underline the phrase that means the most to you. Use the phrase as your special affirmation for manifesting and co-creating throughout this phase of the moon.

I no longer feel the need to be in control and dominated by my mind telling me that it is appropriate to repress my feelings. I am going to claim my dominion today and feel the power of life running through me. I accept the privilege of being fully human and fully alive. I look to see where I lack courage to connect to what is natural for me. I see where I have been stubborn and turn to face my resistance. I become aware where my higher self says "Go" and my lower self says "No." I am aware that my lower self (my body) is a creature of habit and will sabotage me with the idea that change takes too much energy. I take responsibility for the part of me that is a creature of habit and talk to my body about coming into alignment with my new intention to become fully passionate and fully alive. I remember today that in order to get the body to move forward with me, I need two thirds of my cells to align with my request.

First, I become aware of the part of myself that is trying to control all of my outcomes and keep me a slave to those outcomes, rather than trusting in the evolution of nature and the concept of Divine Order. I give up the fight today knowing that this struggle is dissipating all my energy and making me exhausted. In order for my body to respond, I need to awaken my cells through sound and touch. So today, I rub my body and speak out loud by sharing my request for connection, revitalization, rejuvenation, passion, and support. Today, I celebrate the idea that I can connect to my wholeness by activating my cells to support my commitment to my aliveness. I can now stand tall in the center of life and grow in self-confidence.

Leo Homework

Review your memorabilia and see what no longer matches your current love nature, your creative nature, and your loving self. Set your heart free while chanting, "Love is all you need." Become a part of the new consciousness on the Earth that brings a more abundant life when we expand the radius of our love. Live Love Every Day!

Full Moon in Leo

February 14, 3:53 PM

Clearing the Slate for Freedom

Remember a time when you experienced the following trigger points. Write down what happened, forgive yourself, release it, and let it go to clear your slate for freedom.

Impatience

- Forgive
- Release
- Let go

Feeling Superior

- Forgive
- Release
- Let go

Controlling

- Forgive
- Release
- Let go

"Off with Their Heads!" Syndrome

- Forgive
- Release
- Let go

Brat Attacks (Being Childish)

- Forgive
- Release
- Let go

My Freedom List

Leo Freedom List Ideas

Now is the time to set myself free from the need to be the center of attention, obstacles to generosity, false pride and false identity, blocks to confidence and creativity, excuses that keep me from quality time with my children, blocks to knowing that I am loved and lovable, and the idea that everyone needs to be devoted to me in all situations.

Full Moon in Leo

February 14, 3:53 PM

How to Use the Moon Book With Your Chart

Fill in the blanks on the Cosmic Check-In page. Then look up the degree of the moon on the chart below. Take note of the "I" statement on the outside of the wheel where the moon is located. Now locate the same degree on your own chart, and make a note of the house and corresponding "I" statement. Go back to the Cosmic Check-In page and circle the two statements from the charts and read what you wrote. This will give you an idea about what to expect from this moon phase on a personal level.

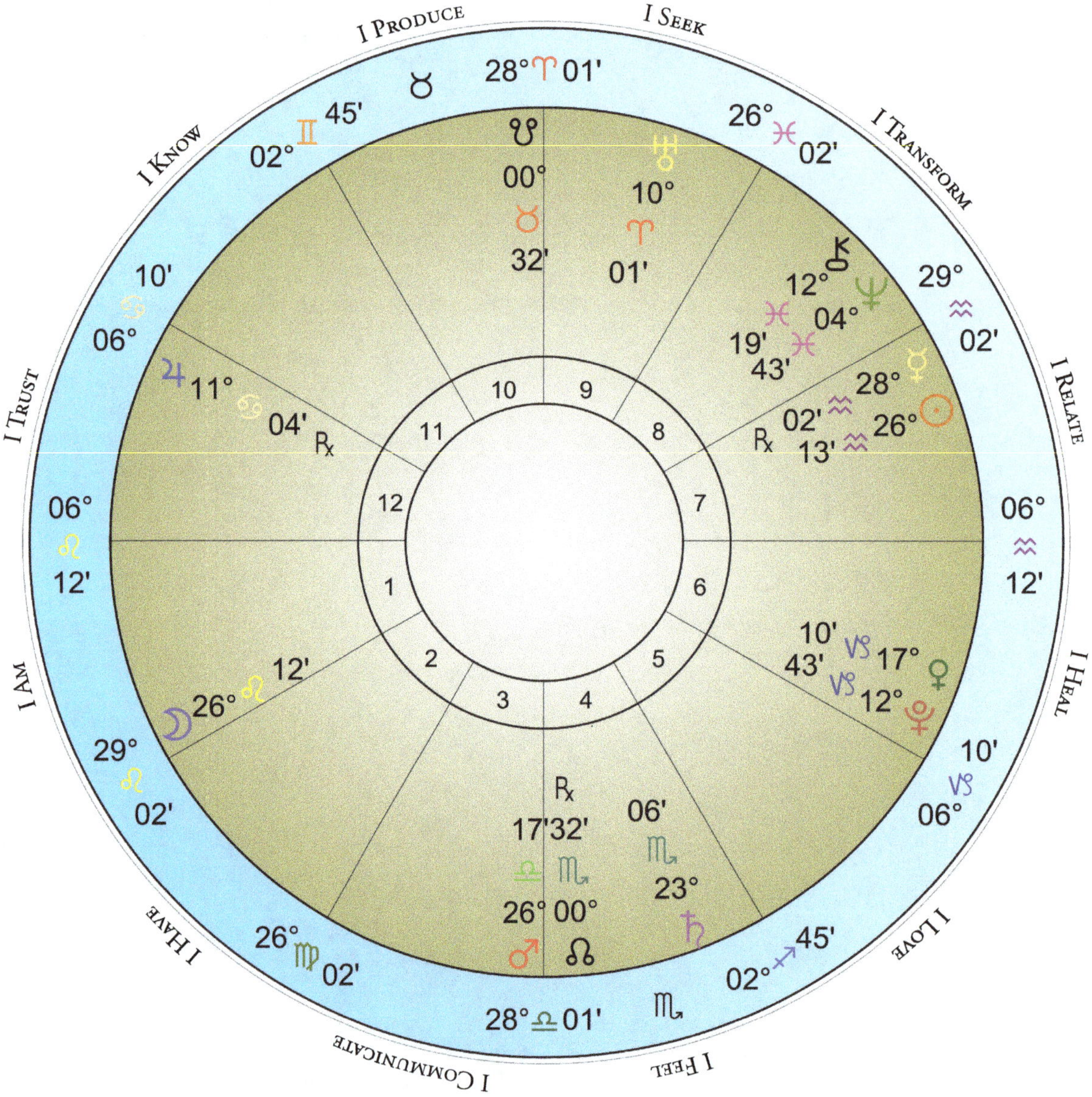

♈ Aries	♋ Cancer	♐ Sagittarius	☽ Moon	♄ Saturn	☊ North Node	V/C Void-of-Course
♉ Taurus	♌ Leo	♑ Capricorn	☿ Mercury	♅ Uranus	☋ South Node	▲ Super-Sensitivity
♊ Gemini	♍ Virgo	♒ Aquarius	♀ Venus	♆ Neptune	➡ Enters	▼ Low-Vitality
	♎ Libra	♓ Pisces	♂ Mars	♇ Pluto	℞ Retrograde	
	♏ Scorpio	☉ Sun	♃ Jupiter	⚷ Chiron	S/D Stationary Direct	

44

Cosmic Check-In

Take a moment to write a brief phrase for each "I" statement.
This activates all areas of your life for this creative cycle.

♌ I Love

♍ I Heal

♎ I Relate

♏ I Transform

♐ I Seek

♑ I Produce

♒ I Know

♓ I Trust

♈ I Am

♉ I Have

♊ I Communicate

♋ I Feel

45

New Moon in Pisces

February 28, 11:59 PM

When the Sun is in Pisces

This is a time when we come in contact with our most Divine essence. It is a time to meditate and connect to your higher purpose. Let your intuition guide you to a program of service. Let your Soul take control and connect to a space beyond your ego. In order to do this, we must become free of our habits, hang ups, and fantasies. Compassion frees us from the slavery of self-interest and the lure of our personality's blind urges, emotional traps, and mental crystallizations. When the Soul takes control, we unite our personality with Divine essence and radiate the light needed to find our true pathway.

Pisces Goddess

Pisces goddess, Kuan Yin, is the embodiment of all that is compassionate. She guides us to the abyss, a place known as emptiness. This place is called the Great Unknown, where the ego drops and there is only the truth of one's nature. Kuan Yin protects us and holds us when we let go, surrender, and evolve. She is the goddess of emptiness. She helps to constantly empty the self from the limitations of the ego—fear, doubt, guilt, shame, and denial. In exchange, we gain beauty, light, and service. She is often pictured riding on the head of a dragon. It is the breath of the dragon that pierces the veil of illusion.

On Your Altar

Colors Turquoise, blue, green, aqua

Numerology 4 – don't overwork a situation

Tarot Card The Moon – the inner journey, reflection, illumination

Gemstones Amethyst, opal, jade, turquoise

Plant Remedy Passion flower – the ability to live in the here and now

Fragrance Lotus – connecting to the Divine without arrogance

Degree Choice Points
  10° Pisces 38'

Motivation Devotion

Resistance Hypocrisy

Statement I Trust
  Body Feet
  Mind Super-sensitive
  Spirit Mystical

Element
  Water – Grace, rhythm, cycles of awareness, Divine Feminine.

Fourth House Moon
  10° Pisces 07'

Motivation Devotion

Resistance Hypocrisy

Fourth House Umbrella Theme
  I Feel – The way your early environmental training was, how that set your foundation for living, and why you chose your mother.

My Co-Creation List

Pisces
Co-Creation Ideas

Now is the time to focus on manifesting connection with the Divine, creativity, healing powers, psychic abilities, sensitivity, compassion, and service.

This, or something better than this, comes to me in an easy and pleasurable way for the good of all concerned. Thank you, Universe!

New Moon in Pisces

February 28, 11:59 PM

Pisces Challenges and Victories

Say all of the statements in this section out loud. Then, underline the phrase that means the most to you. Use the phrase as your special affirmation for manifesting and co-creating throughout this phase of the moon.

I see my path clearly now. I know I must walk by myself on this journey into the deepest part of my Soul. It is time to clear the way and look beneath the surface to discover the parts of myself that I have placed in the unconscious world to be worked on at a later date. That later date is now. I am aware that the postponement of my inner reality can no longer be delayed.

Evolution is pulling me and it has become greater than my distractions, my fear, my denial, and my refusal to face what I have hidden from myself and others. I am aware of outside influences that pull me away from facing my inner realms. I know without a doubt that I am only as sick as the secrets I keep from myself and others. I see clearly how these distractions, illusions, and secrets need to be recognized so I can find the separated parts of myself that have been left in the dark, obscured from the light. I know that it is time to bring myself into wholeness and bring my shadow side to the light of my awareness.

I begin by closing my eyes and experiencing darkness. I imagine myself on a lonely road, in the dark, walking alone. I pay particular attention to the sensations in my body and allow for the body to guide me to the places of dullness, numbness, fear, and anxiety. I simply allow for the intelligence of the body to coordinate the feeling with an image, person, or an event. I stay still and know from the depth of my being that recognition is all that is required of me right now. When recognition occurs, the light of awareness is ignited and the conscious world will take care of the rest. I know that the road to enlightenment requires me to first take the road into the dark side of my Soul.

Pisces Homework

Pisces co-creates by using her psychic powers for counseling, therapy, hypnosis, the ministry, and creating spiritual schools or healing centers. She is also successful in visionary arts, acting, music, medical and pharmaceutical fields, and oceanography.

Take time to go within to discover where new pathways are open for advancement. Blessings pour forth to those who move toward these pathways in the spirit of service. Be open to these pathways and consider the ones that benefit our planet with new ideas, creative expression, and expanded views that lead people to higher levels of service.

Without Acknowledgment Progress Cannot Occur

Acknowledgment creates space for victory and gratitude, which automatically brings us to a level of completion so a new cycle of opportunity can occur in our lives. When we celebrate our wins and acknowledge our victories with gratitude, we update our cells so that our ability to move forward is not hindered by a cellular holographic pattern that is stuck in the past. Cellular lag creates resistance and makes moving forward most difficult. The key is to stay continuously updated by acknowledging yourself for what you did do at the end of each day rather than heading off to sleep thinking about what you did not do. By acknowledging what we didn't do, we play into our karmic storage bank and keep our progress at bay. When we acknowledge ourselves and our manifestations, we are complete, and more cycles of opportunity become available to us in each new day. Be prepared for miracles.

Victory List

Gratitude List

This fulfills the relationship between the giver and the receiver, which completes the cycle with the Universe so that a new beginning can be established.

New Moon in Pisces

February 28, 11:59 PM

How to Use the Moon Book With Your Chart

Fill in the blanks on the Cosmic Check-In page. Then look up the degree of the moon on the chart below. Take note of the "I" statement on the outside of the wheel where the moon is located. Now locate the same degree on your own chart, and make a note of the house and corresponding "I" statement. Go back to the Cosmic Check-In page and circle the two statements from the charts and read what you wrote. This will give you an idea about what to expect from this moon phase on a personal level.

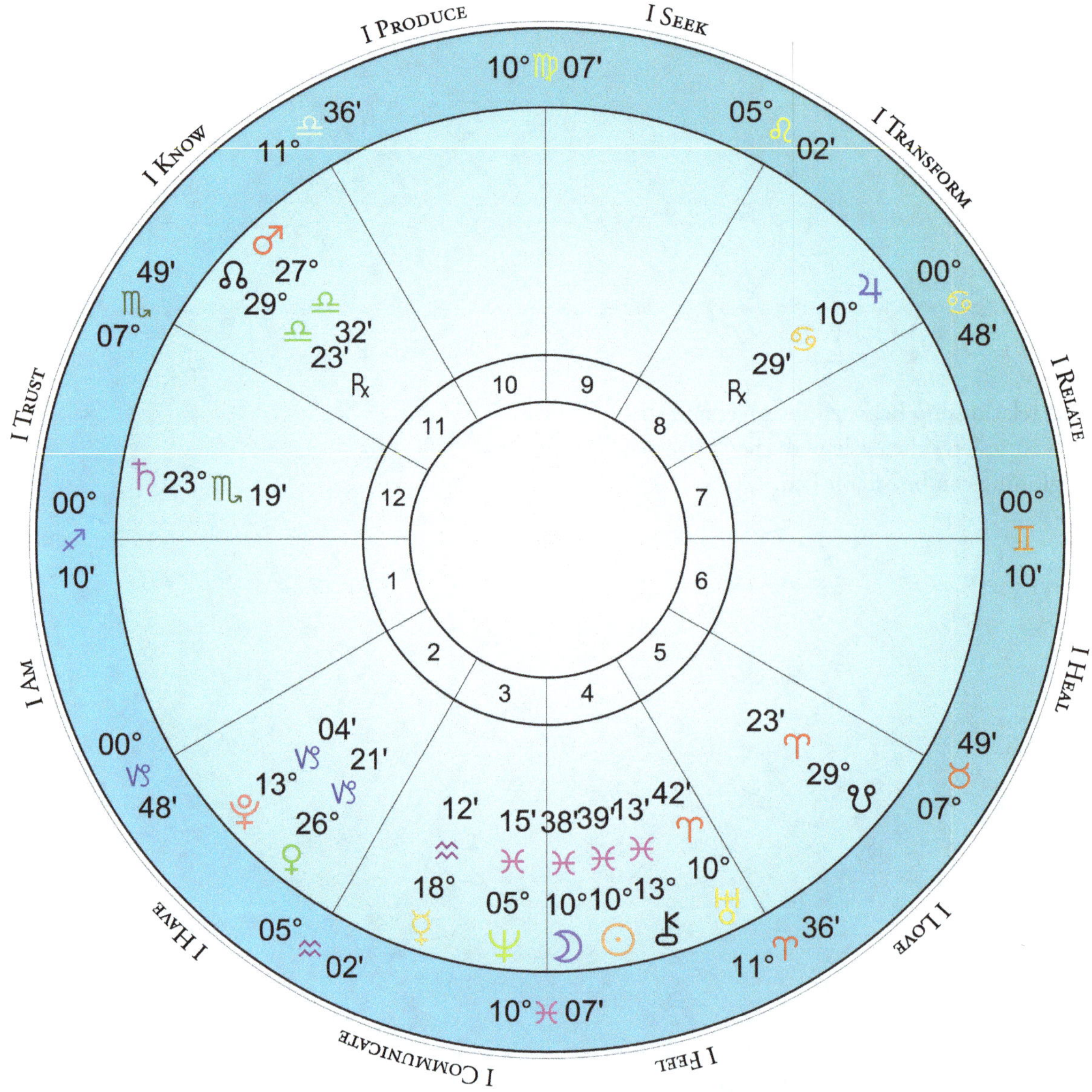

♈	Aries	♋	Cancer	♐	Sagittarius	☽	Moon	♄	Saturn	☊	North Node	V/C Void-of-Course
♉	Taurus	♌	Leo	♑	Capricorn	☿	Mercury	♅	Uranus	☋	South Node	▲ Super-Sensitivity
♊	Gemini	♍	Virgo	♒	Aquarius	♀	Venus	♆	Neptune	➡	Enters	▼ Low-Vitality
		♎	Libra	♓	Pisces	♂	Mars	♇	Pluto	℞	Retrograde	
		♏	Scorpio			☉	Sun	♃	Jupiter	S/D	Stationary Direct	

52

Cosmic Check-In

Take a moment to write a brief phrase for each "I" statement.
This activates all areas of your life for this creative cycle.

♓ I Trust

♈ I Am

♉ I Have

♊ I Communicate

♋ I Feel

♌ I Love

♍ I Heal

♎ I Relate

♏ I Transform

♐ I Seek

♑ I Produce

♒ I Know

March Planetary Highlights

March 1 – Mars goes Retrograde in Libra

Expect to question all action and reaction to any movement that arises. You may try to push the envelope and, because balance is challenged here, accidents could happen. Take time out and do a lot of breath work to keep you calm. Peace will be challenged and the feeling of confinement will become a reality. Do yoga instead of rumba for a while.

March 2 – Saturn goes Retrograde in Scorpio

During this time, it may feel as if someone is watching every move we make; waiting in the wings to make us wrong. It will be important to not be triggered. This is a test for us to see how guilty we feel for something that we have kept under the radar.

March 4 – Jupiter goes Direct in Cancer

We have advanced beyond 2002 and are ready to begin our lives with a new benefits package in the areas of love, health, home, and sex. Be open and ready to receive!

March 5 – Venus Moves into Aquarius

Romance leaves the scene and a more detached approach appears in the love zone. This is a great time to advance our love relationships to a new level and now include friendship. Take on an altruistic project together with your partner and see how well you can make the world a better place as a couple.

March 16 – Mars Retrograde and North Node Retrograde Coupled in Libra

This will be a Spring cleaning for old relationship failures. Make it a clean sweep and recalibrate those times when you blocked love in your life because you had a need to do it all by yourself. Remember that the new relationship paradigm is pulling you towards a new kind of togetherness. Adjust, Accept, Receive, and Acknowledge.

March 17 – Mercury Moves into Pisces

Take an automatic writing course and learn to let Spirit speak through you. Start letting the messages come your way through meditation. Bridge the gap between you and the Divine.

March 20 – The Sun Moves into Aries

This marks the beginning of the Astrological New Year as all of life springs forward awakening us from our Winter sleep. Dreamtime is over and the conscious approach to the year has begun. Wake up and let the games begin!

March 30 – Chiron and Mercury Coupled in Pisces

Let the healing waters of Pisces heal you with words from the Divine. Learn to speak with kindness and compassion by developing a peaceful message.

March 30 – Uranus, Sun, and Moon Conjunct in Aries

This adds some spice to this zesty New Moon. Make space in your life for the unexpected to happen and you may find yourself landing in a garden of delight! Expect visions of your future self to come into view. See if you can freeze-frame the vision and manifest the new you with ease and grace rather than chaos.

Low-Vitality – March 8-9 ▼

This is a time when the Earth is low in energy. Slow down and smell the roses. Going too fast can put your body in jeopardy. Take the time to rest and do what it takes to be kind to yourself and to the Earth. Drink lots of water to keep your body refreshed.

Super-Sensitivity – March 22-23 ▲

This is a time when the global atmosphere is sensitive. Do what you can to avoid the negativity that may be around you. Keep your boundaries clear and stay contained. Beware of your mind taking over and running on overtime.

♈ Aries	♋ Cancer	♐ Sagittarius	☽ Moon	♄ Saturn	☊ North Node	V/C Void-of-Course
♉ Taurus	♌ Leo	♑ Capricorn	☿ Mercury	♅ Uranus	☋ South Node	▲ Super-Sensitivity
♊ Gemini	♍ Virgo	♒ Aquarius	♀ Venus	♆ Neptune	➡ Enters	▼ Low-Vitality
	♎ Libra	♓ Pisces	♂ Mars	♇ Pluto	℞ Retrograde	
	♏ Scorpio	☉ Sun	♃ Jupiter	⚷ Chiron	S/D Stationary Direct	

March

Sunday	Monday	Tuesday	Wednesday	Thursday	Friday	Saturday
						1 ♂♃℞ ♂℞-27°♌32′8:25AM 5. Take a different route today.
2 ♂♄♃℞ ♄℞-23°♏19′8:20AM ☽ V/C 3:03AM ☽→♈ 7:39AM 6. Trust begets trust in friendships.	**3** ♂♄♃℞ 7. Complete your writing project.	**4** ♂♄♃℞ ☽ V/C 9:30AM ☽→♉ 11:12AM 8. Harmony leads to manifestation.	**5** ♂♄♃℞ Ash Wednesday ♀→♒1:04PM 9. Know your emotional needs.	**6** ♂♄℞ ♃D-10°♋26′2:43AM ☽ V/C 5:54AM ☽→♊ 6:37PM 10. Plan a vacation getaway.	**7** ♂♄℞ 2. Balance your finances.	**8** ♂♄℞ ▼ ☽ V/C 11:52PM 3. First of all, believe in yourself.
9 ♂♄℞ ▼ PDT Begins ☽→♋ 6:33AM 4. See yourself centered and balanced.	**10** ♂♄℞ 5. Take a walk in a new area.	**11** ♂♄℞ ☽ V/C 12:50PM ☽→♌ 7:08PM 6. Feel love; be in service today.	**12** ♂♄℞ 7. Mental stimulation is essential.	**13** ♂♄℞ 8. Action creates manifestation.	**14** ♂♄℞ ☽ V/C 12:23AM ☽→♍ 7:17AM 9. Discover the wise person within.	**15** ♂♄℞ 11. Your experience is your truth.
16 ♂♄℞ ○26°♍02′ 10:08 AM ☽ V/C 10:08AM ☽→♎ 5:45PM 3. Create a "play day" with friends.	**17** ♂♄℞ St. Patrick's Day ♀→♓ 3:25PM 4. Be a loyal friend.	**18** ♂♄℞ ☽ V/C 6:06PM 5. Change is the only constant.	**19** ♂♄℞ ☽→♏ 2:13AM 6. Honor your word with love.	**20** ♂♄℞ Spring Equinox ☉→♈ 9:58AM ☽ V/C 8:11PM 7. An open mind sees the brilliance.	**21** ♂♄℞ ☽→♐ 8:38AM 8. See yourself prospering at every turn.	**22** ♂♄℞ ▲ 9. Be a living example of truth.
23 ♂♄℞ ▲ ☽ V/C 3:40AM ☽→♑ 1:03PM 10. Adapting leads to transformation.	**24** ♂♄℞ 2. Consider both instead of either/or.	**25** ♂♄℞ ☽ V/C 5:34AM ☽→♒ 3:38PM 3. Let your joy come alive today.	**26** ♂♄℞ 4. Set the foundation for success.	**27** ♂♄℞ ☽ V/C 6:13AM ☽→♓ 5:10PM 5. Change does assist your growth.	**28** ♂♄℞ 6. Let your authentic self be loved.	**29** ♂♄℞ ☽ V/C 6:43AM ☽→♈ 6:53PM 7. Laughter makes learning easy.
30 ♂♄℞ ●9°♈59′ 11:44 AM 8. We prosper by sharing.	**31** ♂♄℞ ☽ V/C 1:06 PM ☽→♉ 10:20PM 9. Pray for our highest and best good.					

Full Moon in Virgo

March 16, 10:08 AM

The Sun is Opposite the Moon

Full Moons are always in opposition to the Sun. This creates a feeling of tension between where you want to shine and how your feelings are flowing on a sensory level about the Sun's directive. The two forces seem like they are working against each other, yet they are on the same team displaying different techniques to attain the same mission. The Virgo/Pisces polarity creates tension between doing your work and the need to find your path.

Virgo Goddess

Gaia gave birth to herself out of Chaos. After her own birth, she immediately gave birth to Uranus, the King of the Universe. Gaia is the creator of Heaven and Earth. She is the symbol for all that is natural. Unlike her counterpart Uranus, who rules the sky, she rules the womb and enclosed spaces. Gaia is the Earth, giving birth to all of life and all organisms that shape the Earth's biosphere. When the Moon is full in Virgo, we are given the opportunity to look at what we have birthed within ourselves and set ourselves free from what is no longer giving us energy. Virgo sees Divinity in the details, so take a close look at what needs to be released to restore your physical energy.

On Your Altar

Colors Green, blue, earth tones

Numerology 3 – celebrate a "play day" with friends

Tarot Card The Hermit – knowing your purpose and sharing it with the world

Gemstones Emerald, sapphire

Plant remedy Sage – the ability to hold and store light

Fragrance Lavender – management and storage of energy

Degree Choice Points
26° Virgo 01'

Motivation Special privileges

Resistance Appearances

Statement I Heal
  Body Intestines
  Mind Critical
  Spirit Divinity in the details

Element
Earth – Devic communication, green thumb, DNA healing, security, practicality.

Fifth House Moon
10° Virgo 59'

Motivation Mechanical genius

Resistance Familial conformity

Fifth House Umbrella Theme
I Love – The way you love and how you want to be loved.

Meditation

The freedom themes are provided by the zodiac sign and can be from this lifetime or other lifetimes. These meditations assist in dissolving blocks and opening pathways to new frontiers.

When the Moon is in Virgo, the nighttime is sleepless and restless due to mental anxiety coming face-to-face with the thought world. Sit quietly and close your eyes. Breathe in and breathe out. It is a time to discover truth through action, and to detach from pain-producing thinking patterns which lead us to addiction. Ask for an Angel of Records to take you to a moment in time when you chose self-destructive behavior to mask anxiety. Release the addictive thinking patterns that control you. Ask for help from the Angel to see a way to accept the depth of your feelings.

Virgo Challenges and Victories

Say all of the statements in this section out loud. Then, underline the phrase that means the most to you. Use the phrase as your special affirmation for manifesting and co-creating throughout this phase of the moon.

Today I take time to go within to be silent. I imagine myself on a country road moving towards a beautiful mountain. I bask in the glory of the power of the mountain and know that it is calling me to the top. I find a pathway to the top and begin to climb. While I am climbing I become aware of a presence guiding me and empowering me to keep going.

I find a sense of peacefulness in me with this presence. I become aware of my own power in this silent journey to the top and revel in the peacefulness that nature and silence bring me. At last I am about to reach the summit and, just before I do, I feel the power drawing me to go within on a deeper level. I stop for a moment and look back at the path I have just climbed and know that my life's path is a remarkable gift. I connect to the center of the Earth and feel an inner glow.

The top of the mountain calls to me and, as I reach the top, a voice says to me, "Take in the view and look in all directions." I do my 360° turn and, as I do, I sense a light igniting me in every direction. Then the voice says, "Look up!" Now, my awareness shifts and I see that I have become an illuminating light glowing in all six directions. Then the voice says, "Sit in your silence and take in the vastness of who you are. Who you are is immeasurable." I sit, feeling the glow of light within me, and become aware of a greater plan for my life. I allow myself to receive this plan. I accept this assignment and slowly walk down the mountain knowing that I can be a shining light for myself and others. I know I must take my light out to the world and share what I know to be my truth. Today, I become a messenger for the light.

Virgo Homework

Become integrated so that the light of your personality becomes soul-infused. When we are soul-infused and are in service to our higher self, we radiate love and light through the power of the inner self through all activities, thoughts, and emotions and become more magnificent. Learn the art of detachment and let your soul take control.

Full Moon in Virgo

March 16, 10:08 AM

Clearing the Slate for Freedom

Remember a time when you experienced the following trigger points. Write down what happened, forgive yourself, release it, and let it go to clear your slate for freedom.

Judgment

- Forgive
- Release
- Let go

Habitual Actions

- Forgive
- Release
- Let go

Avoiding "The Big Picture" by Being Obsessed with the Details

- Forgive
- Release
- Let go

Being Stubborn

- Forgive
- Release
- Let go

Allowing the Need to Be Perfect to Stop Your Action

- Forgive
- Release
- Let go

My Freedom List

Virgo Freedom List Ideas

Now is the time to set myself free from finding fault with myself, my addiction to perfection, my addiction to detail, over-indulging in image management, pain-producing thinking patterns, judgment of others, resistance to being healthy, and destructive behaviors.

Full Moon in Virgo

March 16, 10:08 AM

How to Use the Moon Book With Your Chart

Fill in the blanks on the Cosmic Check-In page. Then look up the degree of the moon on the chart below. Take note of the "I" statement on the outside of the wheel where the moon is located. Now locate the same degree on your own chart, and make a note of the house and corresponding "I" statement. Go back to the Cosmic Check-In page and circle the two statements from the charts and read what you wrote. This will give you an idea about what to expect from this moon phase on a personal level.

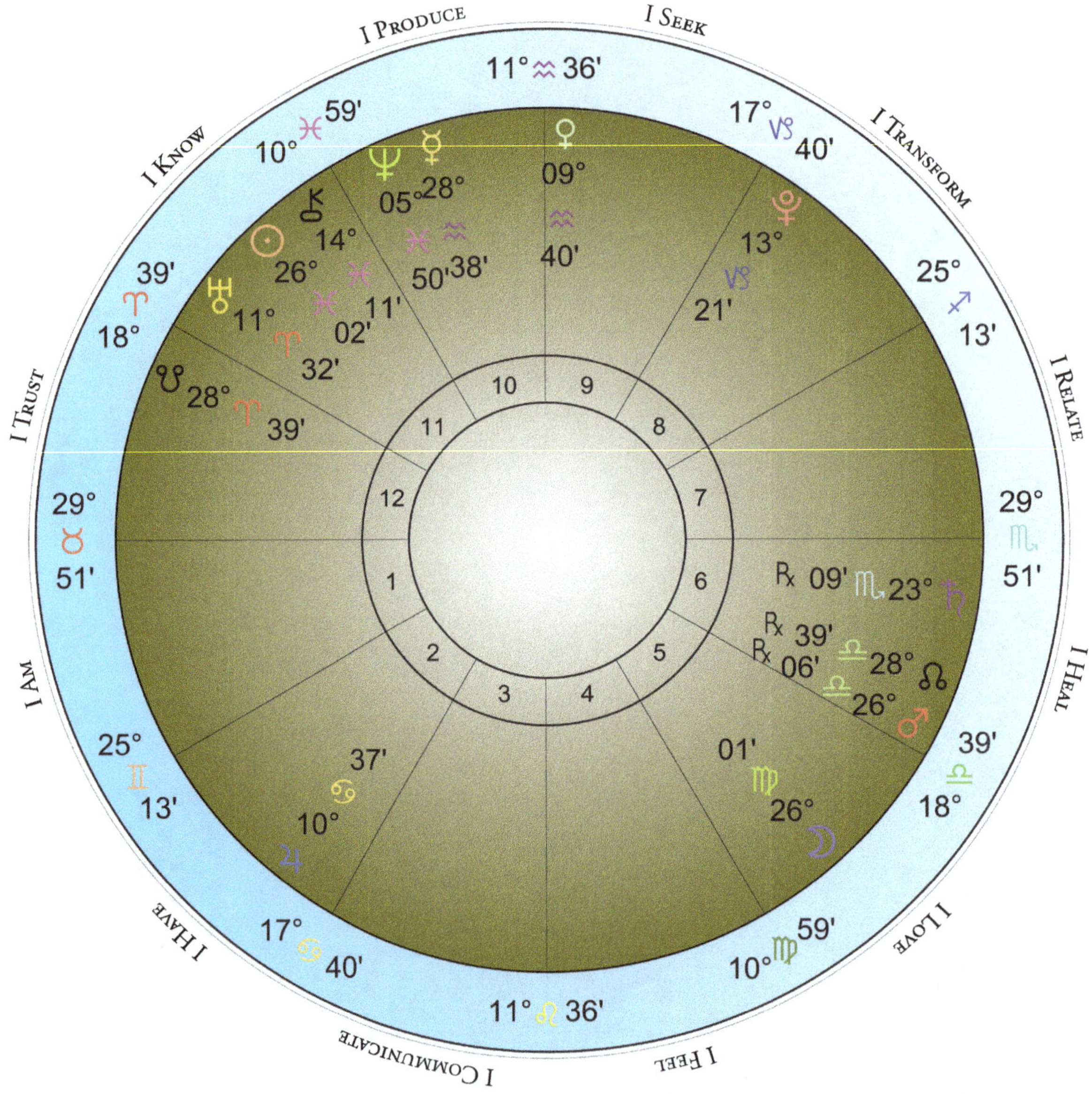

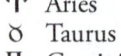

♈ Aries	♋ Cancer	♐ Sagittarius	☽ Moon	♄ Saturn	☊ North Node	V/C Void-of-Course
♉ Taurus	♌ Leo	♑ Capricorn	☿ Mercury	♅ Uranus	☋ South Node	▲ Super-Sensitivity
♊ Gemini	♍ Virgo	♒ Aquarius	♀ Venus	♆ Neptune	➡ Enters	▼ Low-Vitality
	♎ Libra	♓ Pisces	♂ Mars	♇ Pluto	℞ Retrograde	
	♏ Scorpio	☉ Sun	♃ Jupiter	⚷ Chiron	S/D Stationary Direct	

Cosmic Check-In

Take a moment to write a brief phrase for each "I" statement. This activates all areas of your life for this creative cycle.

♍ I Heal

♎ I Relate

♏ I Transform

♐ I Seek

♑ I Produce

♒ I Know

♓ I Trust

♈ I Am

♉ I Have

♊ I Communicate

♋ I Feel

♌ I Love

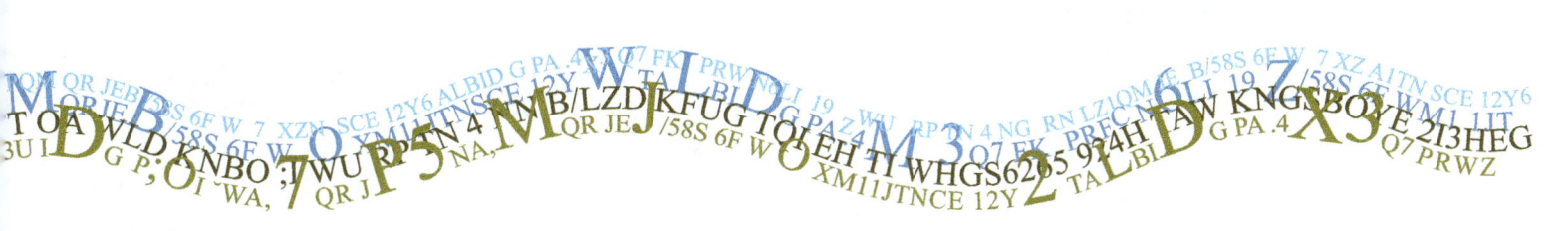

New Moon in Aries

March 30, 11:44 AM

Degree Choice Points
9° Aries 58'

Motivation Reinvigoration

Resistance Distortion

Statement I Am
  Body Head and face
  Mind Ego
  Spirit Awakening

Element
  Fire – Championship energy, serving Self first, Divine Masculine, all-consuming.

Tenth House Moon
  21° Pisces 12'

Motivation Prophecy

Resistance Egotism

Tenth House Umbrella Theme
  I Produce – Your approach to status, career, honor, and prestige, and why you chose your Father.

When the Sun is in Aries

Aries awakens the dreamer from winter sleep and represents the raw energy of Spring, when the new shoots of life burst forth. Aries is the fundamental, straightforward approach to life. There is no challenge that is too great, no obstacle too daunting, and no rival too powerful for the Aries. Aries symbolizes initiation, leadership, strength, and potency. Competition and achievement are very important to Aries. Now is the time to be a pioneer and break all barriers to become the winner you are.

Aries Goddess

Aries goddess, Tara, is the goddess of sublime realization. She assists us in dispelling our fears in order to receive the gifts life has available to us. She was born from a star, sparking life into the dark waters of winter, becoming the first incarnation of water and fire. Thus, the birth of Spring emerges. Legend says that Buddha placed her in the deepest part of the forest to guarantee life and light to all. He claimed her as the Mother of all Buddhas, to be reborn countless lifetimes to guarantee enlightenment and compassion to all women. The Dalai Lama calls her the first "Women's Libber" because she is the symbol of the rebirth of the feminine and gives birth to enlightenment, as does Aries on the equinox.

On Your Altar

Colors Red, black, white

Numerology 8 – we prosper by sharing

Tarot Card Emperor – success on all levels

Gemstones Diamond, red jasper, coral, obsidian

Plant Remedy Pomegranates, oak – planting new life and rooting new life

Fragrance Ginger – the ability to ingest and digest life

My Co-Creation List

Aries Co-Creation Ideas

Now is the time to focus on manifesting personality power, leadership, strength, self-acceptance, winning, courage, personal appearance, and advancing to new frontiers.

This, or something better than this, comes to me in an easy and pleasurable way for the good of all concerned. Thank you, Universe!

New Moon in Aries

March 30, 11:44 AM

Aries Challenges and Victories

Say all of the statements in this section out loud. Then, underline the phrase that means the most to you. Use the phrase as your special affirmation for manifesting and co-creating throughout this phase of the moon.

I am the author of my life. I accept that I am a winner and, in so doing, all doors are open to me. I hold the world in the palm of my hand and I know that there is not a mountain that I cannot climb. My ability to respond to life is in operation today and I direct my intention to bring me to the next level of achievement that I have determined for myself. The world and its systems are available for me to use as tools for my success and I use them with true excellence. I am organized and all systems are in place for me to make my mark on the world. I accept that my structured ground state and my dynamic energy is ready to make headway through pure determination, action, planning, and power. I will manage this plan and know that the sequence of events provided support me to make a breakthrough today.

I am willing to make my plan and take action on it. I gather my support team together today to focus on the appropriate action and encourage each person in their area of excellence and production. I am a great leader and my dynamic power is a good resource for others to determine their own success formula. I am aware that all parts of my team are important and place value on all areas of performance required to manifest in the world. I know how to place people in their best areas of expertise so they can experience their own unique talent manifesting. Today, I honor my father for what he taught me by what he did or didn't do to encourage my ability to perform. I am the producer. I am the protector. I am the provider. I am the promoter. I am power. I am the author of my life.

Aries Homework

Aries co-creates best as a professional athlete, personal trainer or coach, martial arts expert, military professional, demolitions expert, fireworks manufacturer, wardrobe consultant, and through sales and promotions.

Merge your light and dark forces so balance can occur. Then, give shape to your feelings through creative forms and learn to live in the duality of your soul and watch your spirit soar! The embodiment of this duality connects us to the unity, a requirement for these times.

Without Acknowledgment Progress Cannot Occur

Acknowledgment creates space for victory and gratitude, which automatically brings us to a level of completion so a new cycle of opportunity can occur in our lives. When we celebrate our wins and acknowledge our victories with gratitude, we update our cells so that our ability to move forward is not hindered by a cellular holographic pattern that is stuck in the past. Cellular lag creates resistance and makes moving forward most difficult. The key is to stay continuously updated by acknowledging yourself for what you did do at the end of each day rather than heading off to sleep thinking about what you did not do. By acknowledging what we didn't do, we play into our karmic storage bank and keep our progress at bay. When we acknowledge ourselves and our manifestations, we are complete, and more cycles of opportunity become available to us in each new day. Be prepared for miracles.

Victory List

Gratitude List

This fulfills the relationship between the giver and the receiver, which completes the cycle with the Universe so that a new beginning can be established.

New Moon in Aries

March 30, 11:44 AM

How to Use the Moon Book With Your Chart

Fill in the blanks on the Cosmic Check-In page. Then look up the degree of the moon on the chart below. Take note of the "I" statement on the outside of the wheel where the moon is located. Now locate the same degree on your own chart, and make a note of the house and corresponding "I" statement. Go back to the Cosmic Check-In page and circle the two statements from the charts and read what you wrote. This will give you an idea about what to expect from this moon phase on a personal level.

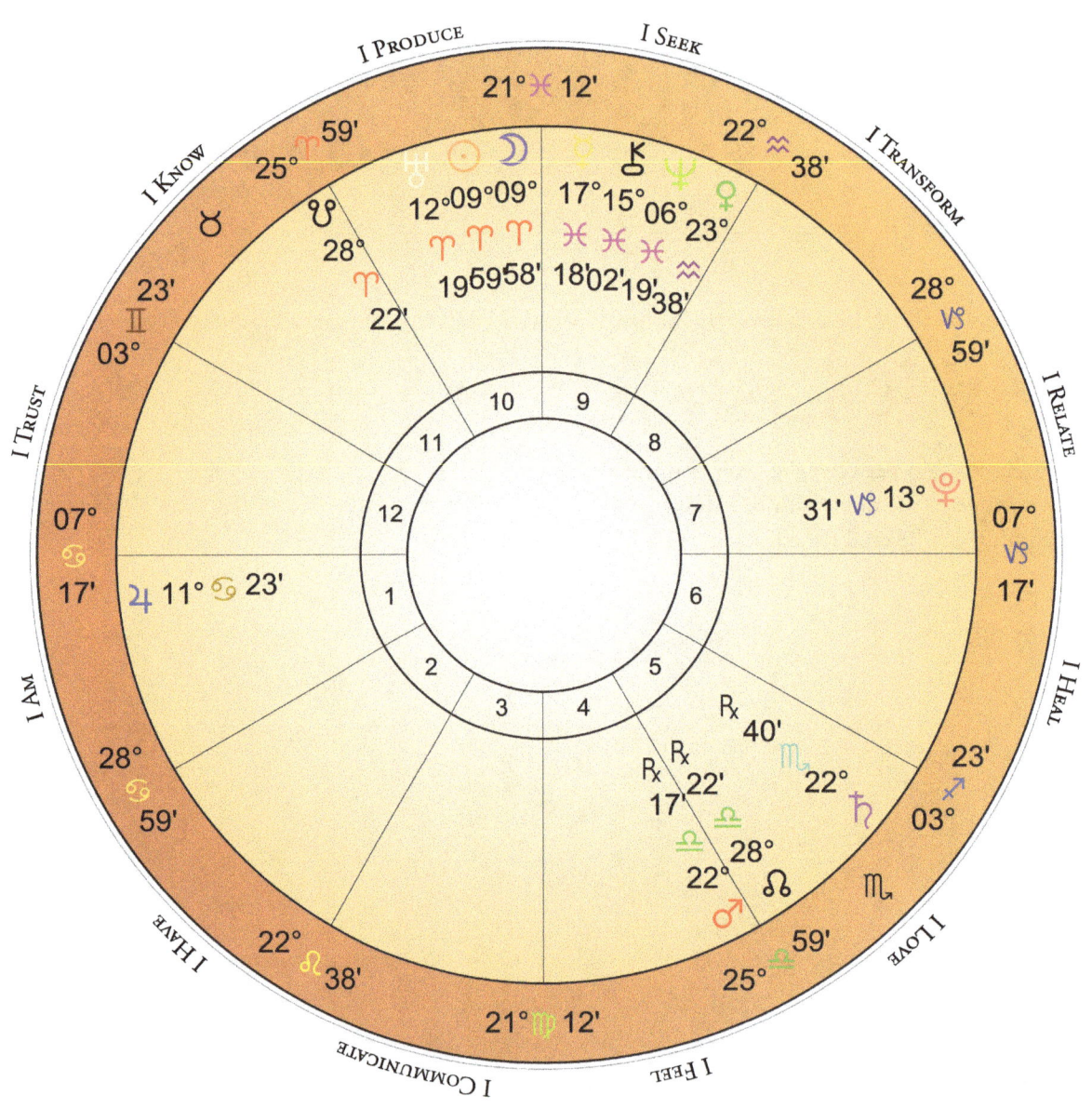

♈ Aries	♋ Cancer	♐ Sagittarius	☽ Moon	♄ Saturn	☊ North Node	V/C Void-of-Course
♉ Taurus	♌ Leo	♑ Capricorn	☿ Mercury	♅ Uranus	☋ South Node	▲ Super-Sensitivity
♊ Gemini	♍ Virgo	♒ Aquarius	♀ Venus	♆ Neptune	➡ Enters	▼ Low-Vitality
	♎ Libra	♓ Pisces	♂ Mars	♇ Pluto	℞ Retrograde	
	♏ Scorpio	☉ Sun	♃ Jupiter	⚷ Chiron	S/D Stationary Direct	

Cosmic Check-In

Take a moment to write a brief phrase for each "I" statement.
This activates all areas of your life for this creative cycle.

♈ I Am

♉ I Have

♊ I Communicate

♋ I Feel

♌ I Love

♍ I Heal

♎ I Relate

♏ I Transform

♐ I Seek

♑ I Produce

♒ I Know

♓ I Trust

April Planetary Highlights

Mars Retrograde in Libra for the Entire Month

Do what you can to keep your mind out of the ego range. If you get an urgent need to "be right," walk away—it will only backfire. Justification will get you in trouble as well.

Jupiter Retrograde in Cancer for the Entire Month

Go to the spa for some nurturing. Take time out this month to do what it takes to feel good. Mother-daughter days will be comforting when you can share special time together shopping or planning a family dinner. Go online and search your family lineage.

April 5 – Venus Enters Pisces

Romance is in the air. Allow yourself time for candles, incense, and a walk on the beach or in the woods. Go dancing, share secrets, and take a chance to be intimate. Read love letters to each other.

April 7 – Mercury Enters Aries

Forging forward will be very easy right now. Take advantage of the speed ratio available to tackle the tasks in true Aries fashion. Mercury will so love that he is the single focus of Aries and you will be happy to get so much accomplished.

April 14 – Pluto goes Retrograde in Capricorn

Yikes! Now is the time to face the money issues that you have been avoiding. Take care of old business and make a priority list. Start at the top of the list to set yourself free.

April 15 – The Moon and North Node Retrograde Conjunct in Libra

Past relationships are up for review now and it's time to see where you allowed yourself to "stick it out" with someone based on survival, rather than love. Look at the concepts that are moving in around the "new" relationship paradigm and do what you can to begin to accept and integrate this new way of loving.

April 15 – Venus and Neptune are Coupled in Pisces

This is where conditional and unconditional love meet and greet each other. Wash away conditions you have placed on yourself, or on your partner, and set the stage for acceptance to begin. Conditional love is being asked to move into the past—see what you can do to make this a reality.

April 15 – Uranus and Mercury are Dancing in Aries

This is a highly-charged field of energy. Expect sudden bursts of energy and ride the current. Choose flexibility and dance into a new, magical place. Resistance at this time leads to exhaustion. Ride the wave!

April 15 – The Sun and the South Node are Together in Aries

The energy is asking us to look at the idea that "doing it alone" is no longer appropriate. This is a time of coming together and leaving behind our single focus that discounted being part of a team. Strength and vulnerability take on a new meaning.

April 19 – The Sun Enters Taurus

It's abundance time! The flowers are blooming and plants are expressing their true nature. Celebrate the beauty in life.

April 23 – Mercury Enters Taurus

Expect to feel like you are walking through yogurt. Mercury loves speed and Taurus loves to "stop and smell the roses." Slow down and enjoy the ride.

April 28 – Pluto in Capricorn and Jupiter in Cancer are Opposed

Pluto strips everything down to the bone so that the truth can emerge. Jupiter, on the other hand, is benevolent, especially while visiting Cancer. Rather than going into conflict here, we must allow Pluto to find the jewels in the truth and allow Jupiter to pour forth the newfound abundance upon us!

Low-Vitality – April 4-5 ▼

This is a time when the Earth is low in energy. Take time out to feel the emotional flow. This will bring you more energy later. Connect with nature and assist the Earth in a healing. Heal yourself as well.

Super-Sensitivity – April 18-19 ▲

This is a time when the global atmosphere is sensitive. This transit accentuates fear rather than freedom globally. Be willing to stay in your own boundaries energetically, so that you stay in the freedom zone. Boundaries on a global level will come into play here and leaders will be stressed.

♈ Aries	♋ Cancer	♐ Sagittarius	☽ Moon	♄ Saturn	☊ North Node	V/C Void-of-Course
♉ Taurus	♌ Leo	♑ Capricorn	☿ Mercury	♅ Uranus	☋ South Node	▲ Super-Sensitivity
♊ Gemini	♍ Virgo	♒ Aquarius	♀ Venus	♆ Neptune	➡ Enters	▼ Low-Vitality
	♎ Libra	♓ Pisces	♂ Mars	♇ Pluto	℞ Retrograde	
	♏ Scorpio	☉ Sun	♃ Jupiter	⚷ Chiron	S/D Stationary Direct	

April

Sunday	Monday	Tuesday	Wednesday	Thursday	Friday	Saturday
		1 ♂ ♄℞ April Fool's Day 10. Don't look back.	2 ♂ ♄℞ ☽ V/C 11:43PM 2. Any decision can be changed.	3 ♂ ♄℞ ☽→♊ 4:47AM 3. You have infinite creative resources.	4 ♂ ♄℞ ▼ 4. Strive to communicate clearly.	5 ♂ ♄℞ ▼ ♀→♓ 1:32PM ☽ V/C 7:55AM ☽→♋ 2:39PM 5. Freely express your vitality.
6 ♂ ♄℞ 6. Friends revitalize you by love.	7 ♂ ♄℞ ☿→♈ 8:36AM ☽ V/C 11:13AM 7. Be stronger than you think you are.	8 ♂ ♄℞ ☽→♌ 2:50AM 8. Respect all living things.	9 ♂ ♄℞ ☽ V/C 11:25PM 9. Live in the moment.	10 ♂ ♄℞ ☽→♍ 3:07PM 10. Renewal is in the now.	11 ♂ ♄℞ 2. Gather facts, then decide.	12 ♂ ♄℞ ☽ V/C 10:11AM 3. Look at it from a different angle.
13 ♂ ♄℞ ☽→♎ 1:33AM 4. The foundation is abundance.	14 ♂ ♄♀℞ Passover ♀℞ 13°♑34′ 4:45PM 5. Change begins with willingness.	15 ♂ ♄♀℞ ○ 25°♎16′ 12:42 AM Lunar Eclipse 12:46AM ☽ V/C 12:42AM ☽→♏ 9:19AM 6. Smile at a stranger today.	16 ♂ ♄♀℞ 7. We teach best by example.	17 ♂ ♄♀℞ ☽ V/C 12:09AM ☽→♐ 2:43PM 8. Give from a generous heart.	18 ♂ ♄♀℞ ▲ 9. Be even more than you are.	19 ♂ ♄♀℞ ▲ ☉→♉ 8:57AM ☽ V/C 6:16PM ☽→♑ 6:27PM 10. Break old patterns.
20 ♂ ♄♀℞ Easter 2. Balance requires action.	21 ♂ ♄♀℞ ☽ V/C 4:20PM ☽→♒ 9:17PM 3. Create beauty in your life.	22 ♂ ♄♀℞ Earth Day 4. Allow for structural change.	23 ♂ ♄♀℞ ☿→♉ 2:17AM ☽ V/C 9:10AM ☽→♓ 11:55PM 5. Find joy in making change.	24 ♂ ♄♀℞ 6. Eliminate a toxic relationship.	25 ♂ ♄♀℞ ☽ V/C 1:02PM 7. Choose to reread a good book.	26 ♂ ♄♀℞ ☽→♈ 3:00AM 8. Abundance is what is.
27 ♂ ♄♀℞ ☽ V/C 4:01AM 9. Make a donation to a charity.	28 ♂ ♄♀℞ Solar Eclipse 11:03 PM ● 8°♉52′ 11:14 PM ☽→♉ 7:23AM 10. Move forward gracefully.	29 ♂ ♄♀℞ 2. Balance requires motion.	30 ♂ ♄♀℞ ☽ V/C 8:53AM ☽→♊ 1:55PM 3. Your creativity has no limits.			

Full Moon in Libra

April 15, 12:42 AM – Lunar Eclipse

Degree Choice Points
  25° Libra 15'

Motivation Power of love

Resistance Conflicting actions

Statement I Relate
  Body Kidneys
  Mind Social
  Spirit Peace

Element
  Air – Need for new insights, active dreaming, freedom from attachments, forgiveness.

Tenth House Moon
  23° Libra 29'

Motivation Curiosity

Resistance Intrusion

Tenth House Umbrella Theme
  I Produce – Your approach to status, career, honor, and prestige, and why you chose your Father.

Karmic Awakening

Childhood issues dealing with collecting what is valued and letting go of what no longer has value.

The Sun is Opposite the Moon

Full Moons are always in opposition to the Sun. This creates a feeling of tension between where you want to shine and how your feelings are flowing on a sensory level about the Sun's directive. The two forces seem like they are working against each other, yet they are on the same team displaying different techniques to attain the same mission. The Libra/Aries polarity creates tension between the idea of "we" versus "me".

Libra Goddess

Athena was born out of her father's head. She was the first woman who incorporated logic into her consciousness. Her keen ability to combine logic and intuition gave birth to strategy. Because of her strategic concepts, she became a consort to all of the great warriors. Unlike Aries, who is the Warrior, Libra is the General. When the Moon is full in Libra, we must look at how strategy is working in our life. Has strategy become out of balance? Are we too removed from "our troops in the field?" It is time to balance our head with our heart.

On Your Altar

Colors Pink, green

Numerology 6 – smile at a stranger today and Live Love!

Tarot Card Justice – the ability to stay in the center of polarity

Gemstones Rose quartz, jade

Plant remedy Olive trees – stamina

Fragrance Eucalyptus – clarity of breath

Meditation

The freedom themes are provided by the zodiac sign and can be from this lifetime or other lifetimes. These meditations assist in dissolving blocks and opening pathways to new frontiers.

When the Moon is in Libra, the ego undergoes a research program looking for motives behind all action. Sit quietly and close your eyes. Breathe in and breathe out. Ask the Angel of Records to take you to a moment in time of perceived errors, miscarriage of justice, or false sense of self-guilt. Ask to be anointed by a cloister of Heavenly Saints so that false guilt can be removed and exchanged for forgiveness. Then a full expression of feelings can flow in a friendly manner toward yourself and others.

Libra Challenges and Victories

Say all of the statements in this section out loud. Then, underline the phrase that means the most to you. Use the phrase as your special affirmation for manifesting and co-creating throughout this phase of the moon.

I am awakened to the reality of the Law of Cause and Effect. I take time out today to see what is coming back to me. I know my actions, my words, and my thoughts have life and manifest in a pattern that returns to me. Today, I am in a place where I can clearly see the results of my words, my actions, and my thoughts. I am aware that it is time for a review and, in so doing, I am given the opportunity to balance, integrate and redistribute these results in a more productive way. When I truly know and experience the Law of Cause and Effect (what I put out comes back to me), I can truly take responsibility for my actions, words, and thoughts, and set myself free of blame. When blame is gone from my thought pattern (self-inflicted blame or circumstantial blame), I am able to benefit from my review rather than wasting energy justifying or defending my position. I now accept the idea that I am free to reconcile with whatever I have labeled as an injustice in my life. I take the time to re-route my thinking towards making life a beneficial experience. Today, I accept that in changing my language I can change my life. Today, I prepare to take actions toward beneficial experiences. Today, I release the need to be right and accept the right to be. Today, I stop judging life and start living life.

Libra Homework

Let the fresh air blow away mental stagnation related to times when you let others' interests supersede your own. Drink an excess amount of water to alert your kidneys that the freedom process has commenced. It's time to deepen your intention to be one with the light, promoting restoration on earth.

Full Moon in Libra

April 15, 12:42 AM – Lunar Eclipse

Clearing the Slate for Freedom

Remember a time when you experienced the following trigger points. Write down what happened, forgive yourself, release it, and let it go to clear your slate for freedom.

Guilt

- Forgive
- Release
- Let go

Need to Justify

- Forgive
- Release
- Let go

Feeling Wrong

- Forgive
- Release
- Let go

Defensive

- Forgive
- Release
- Let go

Avoiding the Moment by Spending Time Strategizing

- Forgive
- Release
- Let go

My Freedom List

Libra Freedom List Ideas

Now is the time to set myself free from situations that are not balanced, people-pleasing and the need to be liked, sorrow over past relationships, unsupportive relationships, the need to be right, false accusations, and being misunderstood.

Full Moon in Libra

April 15, 12:42 AM – Lunar Eclipse

How to Use the Moon Book With Your Chart

Fill in the blanks on the Cosmic Check-In page. Then look up the degree of the moon on the chart below. Take note of the "I" statement on the outside of the wheel where the moon is located. Now locate the same degree on your own chart, and make a note of the house and corresponding "I" statement. Go back to the Cosmic Check-In page and circle the two statements from the charts and read what you wrote. This will give you an idea about what to expect from this moon phase on a personal level.

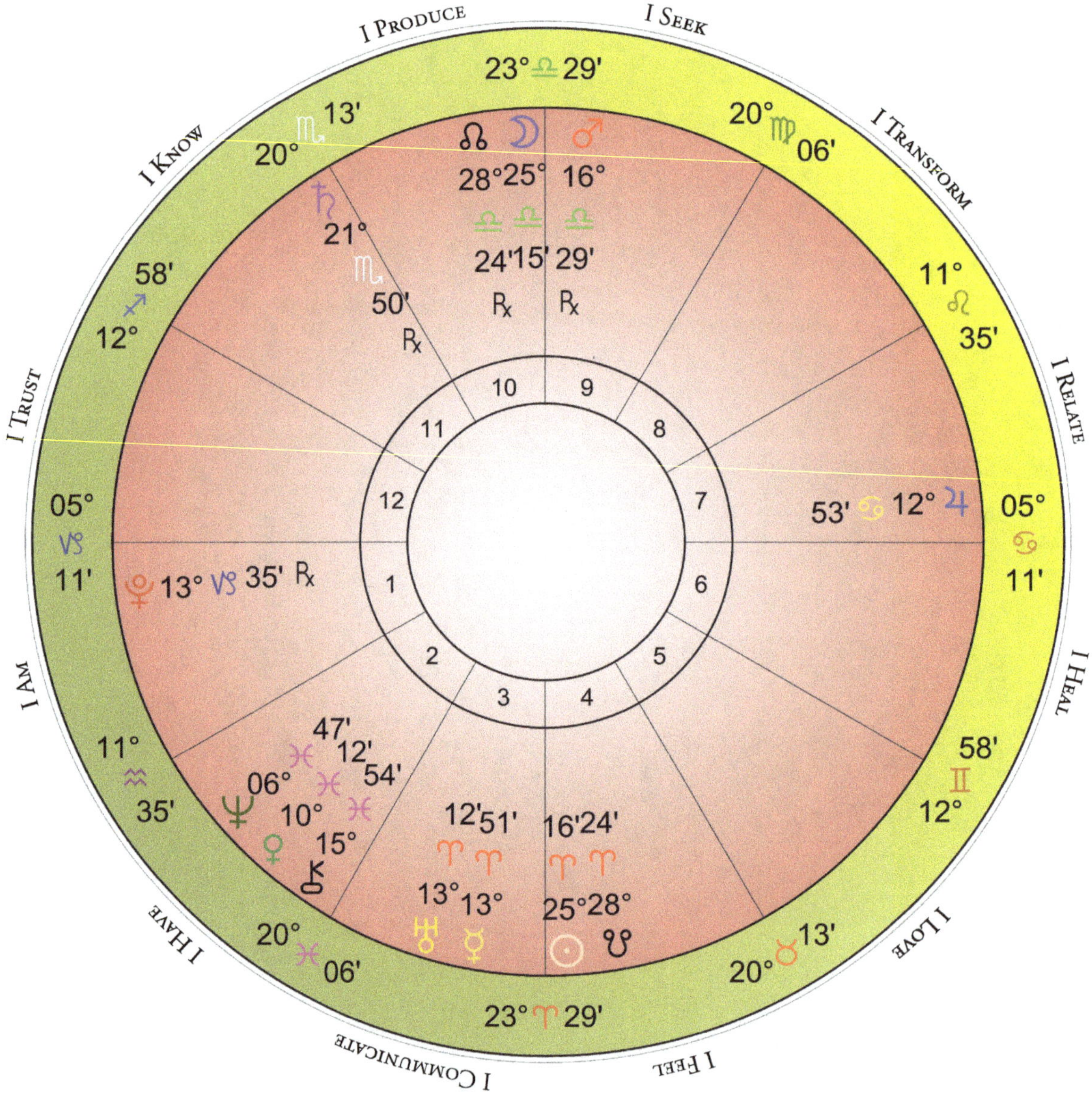

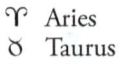

♈ Aries	♋ Cancer	♐ Sagittarius	☽ Moon	♄ Saturn	☊ North Node	V/C Void-of-Course
♉ Taurus	♌ Leo	♑ Capricorn	☿ Mercury	♅ Uranus	☋ South Node	▲ Super-Sensitivity
♊ Gemini	♍ Virgo	♒ Aquarius	♀ Venus	♆ Neptune	➡ Enters	▼ Low-Vitality
	♎ Libra	♓ Pisces	♂ Mars	♇ Pluto	℞ Retrograde	
	♏ Scorpio		☉ Sun	⚷ Chiron	SD Stationary Direct	

Cosmic Check-In

Take a moment to write a brief phrase for each "I" statement. This activates all areas of your life for this creative cycle.

♎ I Relate

♏ I Transform

♐ I Seek

♑ I Produce

♒ I Know

♓ I Trust

♈ I Am

♉ I Have

♊ I Communicate

♋ I Feel

♌ I Love

♍ I Heal

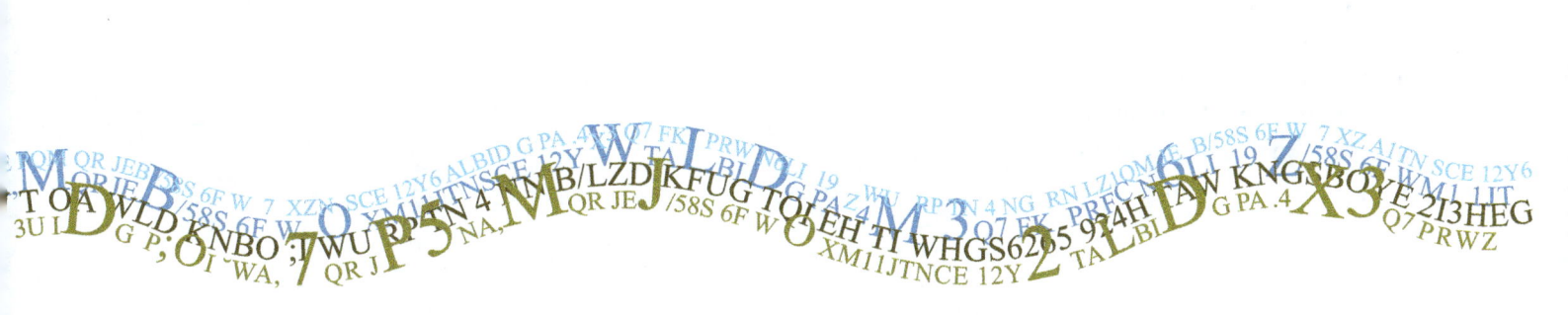

New Moon in Taurus

April 28, 11:14 PM – Solar Eclipse

Degree Choice Points
  8° Taurus 51'

Motivation Loving intent

Resistance Commercialism

Statement   I Have
  Body   Neck
  Mind   Collector
  Spirit Accumulation

Element
  Earth – Acquisition, increasing and creating abundance, practicing generosity.

Fourth House Moon
  14° Aries 38'

Motivation Artful expression

Resistance   Bored with routine

Fourth House Umbrella Theme
  I Feel – The way your early environmental training was, how that set your foundation for living, and why you chose your mother.

Karmic Awakening

We are presented with a choice of living in affluence or living in lack. Remember, you learn about abundance by having it or not having it; the choice is yours.

When the Sun is in Taurus

Taurus is the time when we see the true manifesting power, as the plants move to a higher aspiration of life and bloom. Once again, we become connected to the essence of beauty as a symbol of our divinity. Taurus is the connection between humanity and divinity. Taurus' job is to infuse matter with light through accumulating layers of substance. This is why they are such good shoppers and collectors. The more they accumulate, the more divinity they experience. This process brings about a sense of self-value which is directly commensurate to the amount of money they manifest. Personal resources are part of the pattern. Discover your value at this time.

Taurus Goddess

Taurus goddess, Lakshmi, is the goddess of wealth, abundance, and luxury. Lakshmi is the embodiment of power, fortune, and beauty. She was born out of an ocean of milk. When churned, the alchemy of manifestation turned the milk to butter and a symbol of wealth came into being. She sits on the lotus to remind us to be aware of the stages of evolution required for manifestation, infusing matter with light. Her hands are filled with symbols that show the four stages of manifestation: purpose, wealth, bodily pleasures, and beatitude. The more attention you give Lakshmi in the form of prayer, the wealthier you become.

On Your Altar

Colors Green, pink, deep red, earth tones

Numerology 10 – move forward with grace and ease

Tarot Card Hierophant – the ability to listen, inner-knowing

Gemstones Topaz, agate, smoky quartz, jade, rose quartz

Plant Remedy Angelica – connecting Heaven and Earth

Fragrance Rose – opening the heart

My Co-Creation List

Taurus
Co-Creation Ideas

Now is the time to focus on manifesting success, money, property, luxury, beauty, personal value, and pleasure.

This, or something better than this, comes to me in an easy and pleasurable way for the good of all concerned. Thank you, Universe!

New Moon in Taurus

April 28, 11:14 PM – Solar Eclipse

Taurus Challenges and Victories

Say all of the statements in this section out loud. Then, underline the phrase that means the most to you. Use the phrase as your special affirmation for manifesting and co-creating throughout this phase of the moon.

Everything is possible for me today. My possibilities are endless. I have the power within me to make all of my dreams come true. I have the tools to make my talent a reality. I have the power to identify with my talent. Today, I focus my attention and intention on manifesting with my talent and, in so doing, I transform my ideas into reality. I recognize the part of me that is connected to the cosmic source of ideas and I express that source within me to manifest my creative power. I see my possibilities and act on them today. I am the creative power. I am all-knowing. I am an individual. There is no one else like me. I can manifest anything I desire. I intend it, I allow it, so be it.

Rules for Manifesting

Know what you want. Write it down. Say it out loud. Recognize that because you thought it, it can be so. Release your limiting beliefs. Override your limiting beliefs with power statements. Act as if you have already manifested your idea. Lastly, value yourself!

Taurus Homework

Taurus co-creates best when buying, selling, and owning real estate, gardening and landscaping, selling and collecting art, manufacturing and selling fine furniture, singing or acting, and as a restaurateur, antique dealer, or interior designer.

The Moon in Taurus asks us to infuse light into form and, in so doing, the bridge between humanity and divinity is manifested and we can assume our stewardship in the physical world. When we release Spirit into matter, we become open to the idea that accumulation and actualization set us free to experience the abundance available to us here on Earth. Go shopping!

Without Acknowledgment Progress Cannot Occur

Acknowledgment creates space for victory and gratitude, which automatically brings us to a level of completion so a new cycle of opportunity can occur in our lives. When we celebrate our wins and acknowledge our victories with gratitude, we update our cells so that our ability to move forward is not hindered by a cellular holographic pattern that is stuck in the past. Cellular lag creates resistance and makes moving forward most difficult. The key is to stay continuously updated by acknowledging yourself for what you did do at the end of each day rather than heading off to sleep thinking about what you did not do. By acknowledging what we didn't do, we play into our karmic storage bank and keep our progress at bay. When we acknowledge ourselves and our manifestations, we are complete, and more cycles of opportunity become available to us in each new day. Be prepared for miracles.

Victory List

Gratitude List

This fulfills the relationship between the giver and the receiver, which completes the cycle with the Universe so that a new beginning can be established.

New Moon in Taurus

April 28, 11:14 PM – Solar Eclipse

How to Use the Moon Book With Your Chart

Fill in the blanks on the Cosmic Check-In page. Then look up the degree of the moon on the chart below. Take note of the "I" statement on the outside of the wheel where the moon is located. Now locate the same degree on your own chart, and make a note of the house and corresponding "I" statement. Go back to the Cosmic Check-In page and circle the two statements from the charts and read what you wrote. This will give you an idea about what to expect from this moon phase on a personal level.

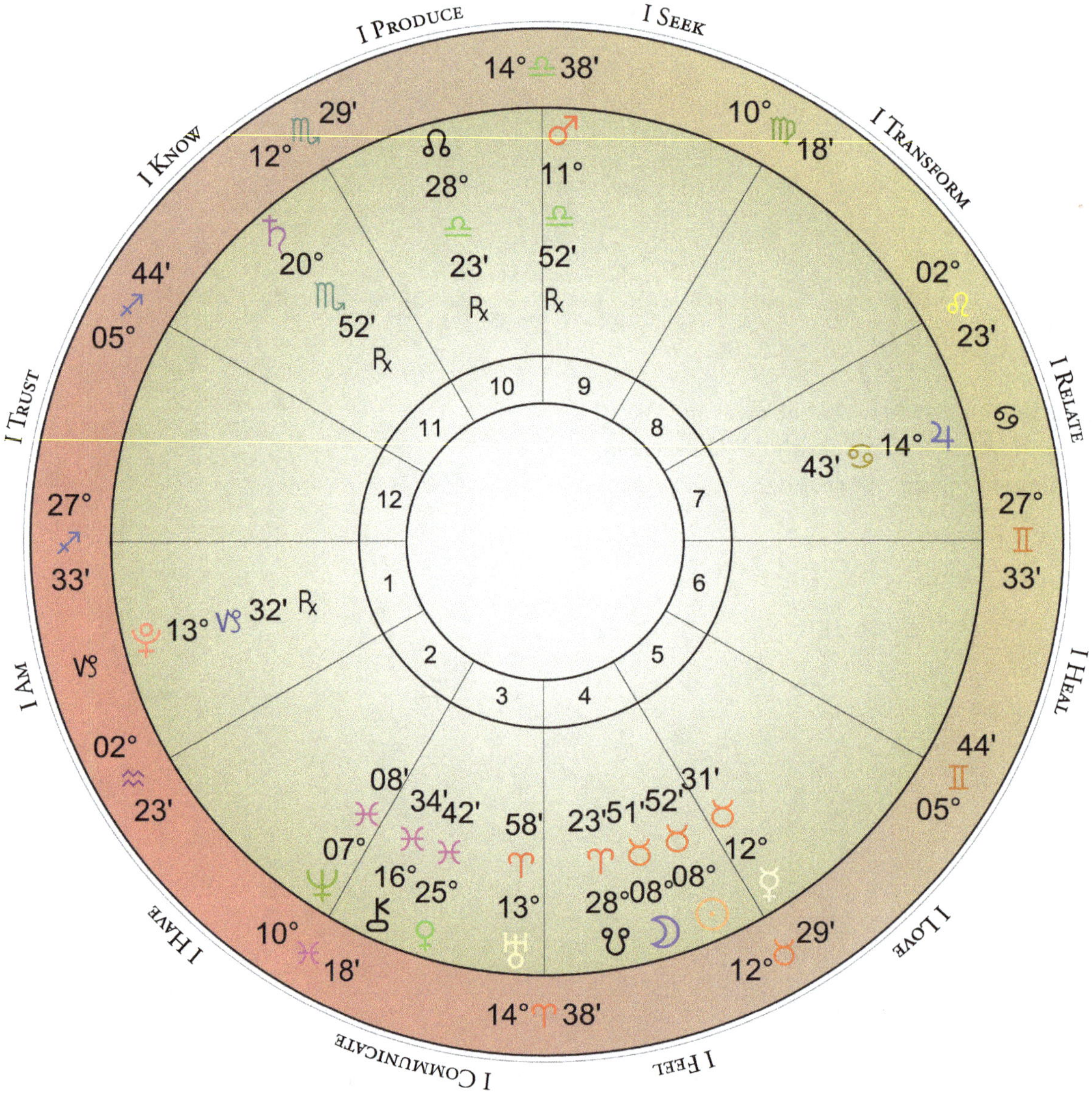

♈ Aries	♋ Cancer	♐ Sagittarius	☽ Moon	♄ Saturn	☊ North Node	V/C Void-of-Course
♉ Taurus	♌ Leo	♑ Capricorn	☿ Mercury	♅ Uranus	☋ South Node	▲ Super-Sensitivity
♊ Gemini	♍ Virgo	♒ Aquarius	♀ Venus	♆ Neptune	➡ Enters	▼ Low-Vitality
	♎ Libra	♓ Pisces	♂ Mars	♇ Pluto	℞ Retrograde	
	♏ Scorpio	☉ Sun	♃ Jupiter	⚷ Chiron	S/D Stationary Direct	

Cosmic Check-In

Take a moment to write a brief phrase for each "I" statement.
This activates all areas of your life for this creative cycle.

♉ I Have

♊ I Communicate

♋ I Feel

♌ I Love

♍ I Heal

♎ I Relate

♏ I Transform

♐ I Seek

♑ I Produce

♒ I Know

♓ I Trust

♈ I Am

May Planetary Highlights

Mars Retrograde in Libra Until May 19

Don't even try to make a decision during this time. The contrary aspects of Libra can exhaust the mind with Mars' need for action. Use the power of Mars to activate your mind to find solutions to peace on Earth. Put the diplomacy of Libra to work solving problems, rather than making war.

Saturn Retrograde in Scorpio for the Entire Month

Exposure is in the air. Secrets are unfolding in several areas beyond your wildest imagination. This is necessary for our development as a society, so enjoy the show. Hold space for purification and healing, rather that getting judgmental and pushing the secrets back under the rug.

Pluto Retrograde in Capricorn for the Entire Month

Systems are changing and foundations are crumbling. Hold space for this to be constructive rather than destructive—the faster it happens the better our lives will be. Know that Pluto is in search of truth, so that we can re-build our lives in a conscious, Co-Creative way.

May 2 – Venus Enters Aries

Immediate gratification takes over here and could be unsettling if immediate results don't happen right away. This fast pace can lead you down new love pathways, and some fun can happen if you go with the flow. Don't push the river, simply flow with it and your love life will be filled with excitement.

May 7 – Mercury Enters Gemini

This is a great time for lively conversations! Let your mind interact with those around you and know that these ideas can become reality if worked correctly. That sales pitch you have been waiting to present will have awesome results right now. Travel will be wonderful and easy. Go to parties where inspirational people are and sail off into the sunset with flirting, joking, and sharing ideas. It's time for your mind to shine!

May 14 – Saturn is Dancing with the Moon in Scorpio

Mom and Dad are dancing together here. It's time to look at how your mother motivated you to value yourself by what she did or didn't do. Do the same with your Dad—how did he motivate you to produce in the world by what he did or didn't do? This process can be very healing if you are willing to play the game.

May 14 – Venus and Uranus are Coupled in Aries

Expect a wild and unusual love interest to come forward and add some spice in your life. There is an urge here for something new to happen in the relationship area. Enjoy the ride!

May 20 – The Sun Enters Gemini

Time to get your message out into the marketplace. The goal here is to become aware of your unique characteristics and capitalize on them. Travel is also in the air—make sure that you have a place in mind and go there. Start or join a discussion group on a subject of interest and expand your mind.

May 28 – Venus and the South Node are Connecting in Aries

This is where Femininity takes a look at the past and re-evaluates what is needed to make a new kind of splash to recalibrate herself in relationship to her man-self.

May 29 – Mercury Enters Cancer

Time to communicate with the family and get it right this time! Work on compassionate ways to relate, so that the idea of family can take on a new twist for you.

Low-Vitality – May 1, 2, 29-30 ▼

This is a time when the Earth is in a low energy pocket. It's best to conserve your energy, get rest, or do special nurturing things for yourself and your family. Earth changes are possible during these days, so stay close to home.

Super-Sensitivity – May 16-17 ▲

This is a time when the global atmosphere is sensitive. Watch out for obsessive thinking that can damage your self-esteem. Keep your ego from overloading your mind with judgments and devaluation. Become aware of punishing thoughts; they could backfire.

♈ Aries	♋ Cancer	♐ Sagittarius	☽ Moon	♄ Saturn	☊ North Node	V/C Void-of-Course
♉ Taurus	♌ Leo	♑ Capricorn	☿ Mercury	♅ Uranus	☋ South Node	▲ Super-Sensitivity
♊ Gemini	♍ Virgo	♒ Aquarius	♀ Venus	♆ Neptune	➡ Enters	▼ Low-Vitality
	♎ Libra	♓ Pisces	♂ Mars	♇ Pluto	℞ Retrograde	
	♏ Scorpio	☉ Sun	♃ Jupiter	⚷ Chiron	S/D Stationary Direct	

May

Sunday	Monday	Tuesday	Wednesday	Thursday	Friday	Saturday
				1 ♂ ♄♀℞ ▼ May Day ☽ V/C 4:31PM 4. Health requires discipline.	**2** ♂ ♄♀℞ ▼ ♀→♈ 6:22PM ☽→♋ 11:12PM 5. Resisting change is pointless.	**3** ♂ ♄♀℞ 6. See the humor in what you do.
4 ♂ ♄♀℞ 7. Look deeply within and release.	**5** ♂ ♄♀℞ Cinco de Mayo ☽ V/C 1:45AM ☽→♌ 10:55 AM 8. Celebrate your successful actions.	**6** ♂ ♄♀℞ 9. Spirituality awakens physical action.	**7** ♂ ♄♀℞ ☿→♊ 7:58AM ☽ V/C 3:50AM ☽→♍ 11:23PM 10. Recycling the past is pointless.	**8** ♂ ♄♀℞ 11. Use your mystical awareness.	**9** ♂ ♄♀℞ ☽ V/C 3:08PM 3. Scatter joy everywhere you go.	**10** ♂ ♄♀℞ ☽→♎ 10:18AM 4. Be someone others can depend on.
11 ♂ ♄♀℞ Mother's Day ☽ V/C 5:50PM 5. Handle the moment and move on.	**12** ♂ ♄♀℞ ☽→♏ 6:06PM 6. Enjoy your sensuality. It is a gift.	**13** ♂ ♄♀℞ 7. Smart is good. Wise is better.	**14** ♂ ♄♀℞ ○ 23°♏55′ 12:15 PM ☽ V/C 12:15PM ☽→♐ 10:43PM 8. Learn to be self-sufficient.	**15** ♂ ♄♀℞ 9. Feel the fire of heavenly love.	**16** ♂ ♄♀℞ ▲ ☽ V/C 12:43AM 10. A new direction may be in order.	**17** ♂ ♄♀℞ ▲ ☽→♑ 1:11AM 11. Be one with all of life.
18 ♂ ♄♀℞ 3. Create a surprise for someone.	**19** ♄♀℞ ♂☋ 9°♌01′ 6:32PM ☽ V/C 12:02AM ☽→♒ 2:57AM 4. Structure helps us stay on purpose.	**20** ♄♀℞ ☉→♊ 8:00PM ☽ V/C 3:21PM 5. Go out and play with a friend.	**21** ♄♀℞ ☽→♓ 5:18AM 6. The body is a temple for spirit.	**22** ♄♀℞ ☽ V/C 11:25PM 7. Teach something you know.	**23** ♄♀℞ ☽→♈ 9:01AM 8. Be sure to value who you are.	**24** ♄♀℞ 9. Allow your radiance to shine.
25 ♄♀℞ ☽ V/C 8:57AM ☽→♉ 2:27PM 10. Think up your dream vacation.	**26** ♄♀℞ Memorial Day 11. Build a magnetic field.	**27** ♄♀℞ ☽ V/C 2:09AM ☽→♊ 9:47PM 4. Your strength supports others.	**28** ♄♀℞ ● 7°♊21′ 11:40AM 5. Help someone make a change.	**29** ♄♀℞ ▼ ☿→♋ 2:13AM ♀→♉ 6:47PM ☽ V/C 2:58AM 6. You have the ability to heal.	**30** ♄♀℞ ▼ ☽→♋ 7:13AM 7. Learn something new today.	**31** ♄♀℞ ☽ V/C 11:32PM 8. New awareness creates abundance.

Full Moon in Scorpio

May 14, 12:15 PM

Degree Choice Points
23° Scorpio 53'

Motivation	Grounded instruction
Resistance	Condescension
Statement	I Transform
Body	Reproductive organs
Mind	Investigation
Spirit	Transformation

Element
Water – Seeks lowest ground to be contained, all-consuming emotions, need for soul nourishment, sensitivity to others.

Fourth House Moon
16° Scorpio 31'

Motivation	Creating your reality
Resistance	Overly-responsible

Fourth House Umbrella Theme
I Feel – The way your early environmental training was, how that set your foundation for living, and why you chose your mother.

The Sun is Opposite the Moon

Full Moons are always in opposition to the Sun. This creates a feeling of tension between where you want to shine and how your feelings are flowing on a sensory level about the Sun's directive. The two forces seem like they are working against each other, yet they are on the same team displaying different techniques to attain the same mission. The Scorpio/Taurus polarity creates tension between feeling deeply about shared resources and living abundantly for yourself.

Scorpio God

Pluto was one of the three remaining sons of Saturn who were not consumed by his wrath. The three brothers looked at the elements that Time could not consume: Air, Water, and Death. The three brothers chose their non-consumable domains. Jupiter took the air, Neptune the water, and Pluto the grave or the underworld. Pluto means wealth in the Greek language and is defined as "invisible fullness." Pluto is the god of wealth. Hidden assets belong to the underworld and cannot be consumed until they are brought above the ground. When the Moon is full in Scorpio, we are given the opportunity to shine the light on our own underworld and see what we are hiding on an unconscious level. Subjects that Pluto tends to keep hidden are death, taxes, money, legacies, and sex. Look deep within yourself to see what resentments, fears, or hidden agendas you might be harboring in these areas. Bring them forward above the ground and into the light of day.

On Your Altar

Colors Indigo, deep purple, scarlet

Numerology 8 – money, power, and success

Tarot Card Death – the ability to make changes

Gemstones Topaz, tanzanite, onyx, obsidian

Plant remedy Manzanita – prepares the body for transformation

Fragrance Sandalwood – awakens your sensuality

Meditation

The freedom themes are provided by the zodiac sign and can be from this lifetime or other lifetimes. These meditations assist in dissolving blocks and opening pathways to new frontiers.

When the Moon is in Scorpio, it is time to contact an Angel of Transformation to move you beyond the unruly representatives of your lower nature, such as retaliation, revenge, dominance, and misappropriated sexual focus.

Sit down quietly. Breathe in and breathe out. Ask for clarification of purpose and dedication without deviation. Work with the Angel of Transformation to assist you in freeing yourself from any judgment attached to indiscretions, and replace your field of awareness with appropriate focus, determination, and drive.

Scorpio Challenges and Victories

Say all of the statements in this section out loud. Then, underline the phrase that means the most to you. Use the phrase as your special affirmation for manifesting and co-creating throughout this phase of the moon.

I will not compromise myself today. I know that transformation occurs when I stand tall in my truth, even if everything around me needs to die. I see death as a new beginning and know that in death comes new aliveness. I am willing to embrace transformation and open to the idea that change is in my favor. I know that in letting go, I give new life to myself. I am willing to accept that life is ever-changing and in a constant state of renewal; one cannot occur without the other.

Releasing is easy when I offer myself something new. When I allow for the motion of change to stay alive, I let go with one hand and receive with the other hand. The ever-present flow and motion keeps me alive and connected to the revitalizing power of Nature. When the power of Nature becomes apparent to me, I become aware that Nature abhors a vacuum. Rejuvenation is mine when I embrace change.

Scorpio Homework

The Scorpio Moon creates the urge within us to make life happen. Pay attention to these urges so you can prepare yourself toward greater action, intention, and purpose.

Full Moon in Scorpio

May 14, 12:15 PM

Clearing the Slate for Freedom

Remember a time when you experienced the following trigger points. Write down what happened, forgive yourself, release it, and let it go to clear your slate for freedom.

Secrets

- Forgive
- Release
- Let go

Sharing Money

- Forgive
- Release
- Let go

Sexual Indiscretions

- Forgive
- Release
- Let go

Control Dramas

- Forgive
- Release
- Let go

Revenge

- Forgive
- Release
- Let go

My Freedom List

Scorpio Freedom List Ideas

Now is the time to set myself free from resentment, jealousy, revenge, joint financial situations, vendettas, betrayals, blocks to transformation, destructive relationships, resistance to changing paradigms, obstacles to having a healthy sex life, karma relating to all issues of power.

Full Moon in Scorpio

May 14, 12:15 PM

How to Use the Moon Book With Your Chart

Fill in the blanks on the Cosmic Check-In page. Then look up the degree of the moon on the chart below. Take note of the "I" statement on the outside of the wheel where the moon is located. Now locate the same degree on your own chart, and make a note of the house and corresponding "I" statement. Go back to the Cosmic Check-In page and circle the two statements from the charts and read what you wrote. This will give you an idea about what to expect from this moon phase on a personal level.

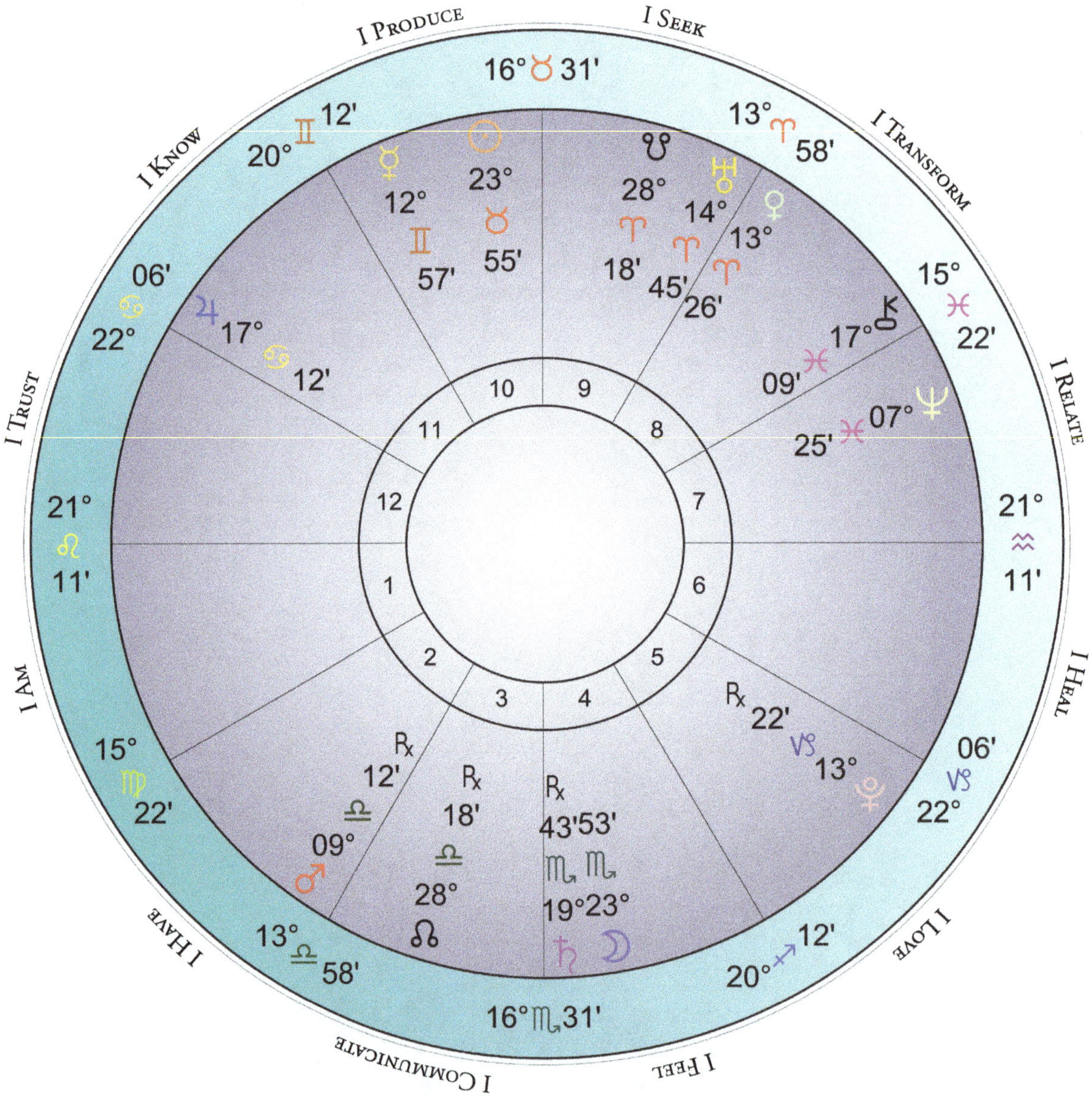

♈ Aries	♋ Cancer	♐ Sagittarius	☽ Moon	♄ Saturn	☊ North Node	V/C Void-of-Course
♉ Taurus	♌ Leo	♑ Capricorn	☿ Mercury	⛢ Uranus	☋ South Node	▲ Super-Sensitivity
♊ Gemini	♍ Virgo	♒ Aquarius	♀ Venus	♆ Neptune	➡ Enters	▼ Low-Vitality
	♎ Libra	♓ Pisces	♂ Mars	♇ Pluto	℞ Retrograde	
	♏ Scorpio	☉ Sun	♃ Jupiter	⚷ Chiron	S/D Stationary Direct	

Cosmic Check-In

Take a moment to write a brief phrase for each "I" statement.
This activates all areas of your life for this creative cycle.

♏ I Transform

♐ I Seek

♑ I Produce

♒ I Know

♓ I Trust

♈ I Am

♉ I Have

♊ I Communicate

♋ I Feel

♌ I Love

♍ I Heal

♎ I Relate

New Moon in Gemini

May 28, 11:40 AM

When the Sun is in Gemini

This is a time when the ability to communicate is at the top of the priority list. Allow your thoughts to lead you to a formula for success so you can put your thoughts into action. Then, find the appropriate soapbox to stand on so your message can be heard. Right now is the time to make your message clear, enlightening, witty, and thought-provoking. Your bright mind is at its high throne and waiting for an audience. Try blogging, do a show on YouTube, join Toast Masters, write that screenplay, film yourself doing a travel show, start a discussion group, or write a newsletter for your neighborhood. Most of all, put your bright mind to work!

Gemini Goddess

Maya is the goddess of illusion. She tempts the mind into believing that what it thinks is always correct. She challenges you every step of the way to learn where the ego kicks in and leads you down pathways that are destructive. Her constant "mind chatter" sounds so convincing that one can spend an entire life living the illusion that thinking is better than experiencing. Maya will build this illusion so deep in the mind that you actually believe that your thoughts are worthy of accolades in the outer world. She distorts the value of inner work to keep you from knowing your personal truth.

On Your Altar

Colors Bright yellow, orange, multi-colors

Numerology 5 – make a change today, add variety into your life

Tarot Card Lovers – connecting to wholeness

Gemstones Yellow diamond, citrine

Plant Remedy Morning Glory – thinking with your heart not your head

Fragrance Iris – the ability to focus the mind

Degree Choice Points
7° Gemini 21'

Motivation Negotiation

Resistance Social inequity

Statement I Communicate
Body Lungs and hands
Mind Intellect
Spirit Intelligence

Element
Air – Freedom from attachment, curiosity, flexibility, active dreaming, bridge between the mundane and spiritual worlds.

Tenth House Moon
21° Taurus 30'

Motivation Discernment

Resistance Blind obedience

Tenth House Umbrella Theme
I Produce – Your approach to status, career, honor, and prestige, why you chose your Father.

My Co-Creation List

Gemini
Co-Creation Ideas

Now is the time to focus on manifesting communications, a promotion, technology, ideas, non-judgmental communication, thinking outside of duality, a quiet mind, charisma and charm, and flirting.

This, or something better than this, comes to me in an easy and pleasurable way for the good of all concerned. Thank you, Universe!

New Moon in Gemini

May 28, 11:40 AM

Gemini Challenges and Victories

Say all of the statements in this section out loud. Then, underline the phrase that means the most to you. Use the phrase as your special affirmation for manifesting and co-creating throughout this phase of the moon.

I am dark. I am light. I am day. I am night. The extremes in life exist within me, completing themselves in reality. The "I" that is "we" lives within me. I am one in the same. I am both.

I know that flow comes from accepting my opposite natures. Today, I accept my opposites and get into the flow. I am aware today of how my judgments separate me from people, events, experiences, and, most of all, from myself. Today, I am going to see where I have separated all of the parts of myself and begin to integrate into wholeness through acceptance and understanding. I begin by breathing. I breathe in wholeness and breathe out separation. I understand that breath is life and that life includes all facets of my experience to gain awareness. I know that I am Heaven. I know that I am Earth. I know that I am masculine. I know that I am feminine. Today, I become unified. Today, I integrate into wholeness. I breathe into all of these aspects of myself, knowing that in my totality I am connected to Oneness. The "I" that is "we" lives within me. I am one in the same. I am both.

Gemini Homework

The Gemini co-creates best through broadcasting and journalism, as a speech coach, comedian, political satirist, gossip columnist, negotiator, media specialist, manicurist, salesperson, teacher, or travel consultant.

Expect to awaken your will on seven levels…

- The will to direct – through the power of your original intention.
- The will to love – stimulating goodwill among humankind through cooperation.
- The will to act – by laying foundations for a happier world.
- The will to cooperate – the desire and demand for right relationships.
- The will to know – to think correctly and creatively so that every man/woman can find their outstanding characteristics.
- The will to persist – to be one with your light and represent the ideal standard for living.
- The will to organize – to carry forward direct inspiration through groups of goodwill.

Without Acknowledgment Progress Cannot Occur

Acknowledgment creates space for victory and gratitude, which automatically brings us to a level of completion so a new cycle of opportunity can occur in our lives. When we celebrate our wins and acknowledge our victories with gratitude, we update our cells so that our ability to move forward is not hindered by a cellular holographic pattern that is stuck in the past. Cellular lag creates resistance and makes moving forward most difficult. The key is to stay continuously updated by acknowledging yourself for what you did do at the end of each day rather than heading off to sleep thinking about what you did not do. By acknowledging what we didn't do, we play into our karmic storage bank and keep our progress at bay. When we acknowledge ourselves and our manifestations, we are complete, and more cycles of opportunity become available to us in each new day. Be prepared for miracles.

Victory List

Gratitude List

This fulfills the relationship between the giver and the receiver, which completes the cycle with the Universe so that a new beginning can be established.

New Moon in Gemini

May 28, 11:40 AM

How to Use the Moon Book With Your Chart

Fill in the blanks on the Cosmic Check-In page. Then look up the degree of the moon on the chart below. Take note of the "I" statement on the outside of the wheel where the moon is located. Now locate the same degree on your own chart, and make a note of the house and corresponding "I" statement. Go back to the Cosmic Check-In page and circle the two statements from the charts and read what you wrote. This will give you an idea about what to expect from this moon phase on a personal level.

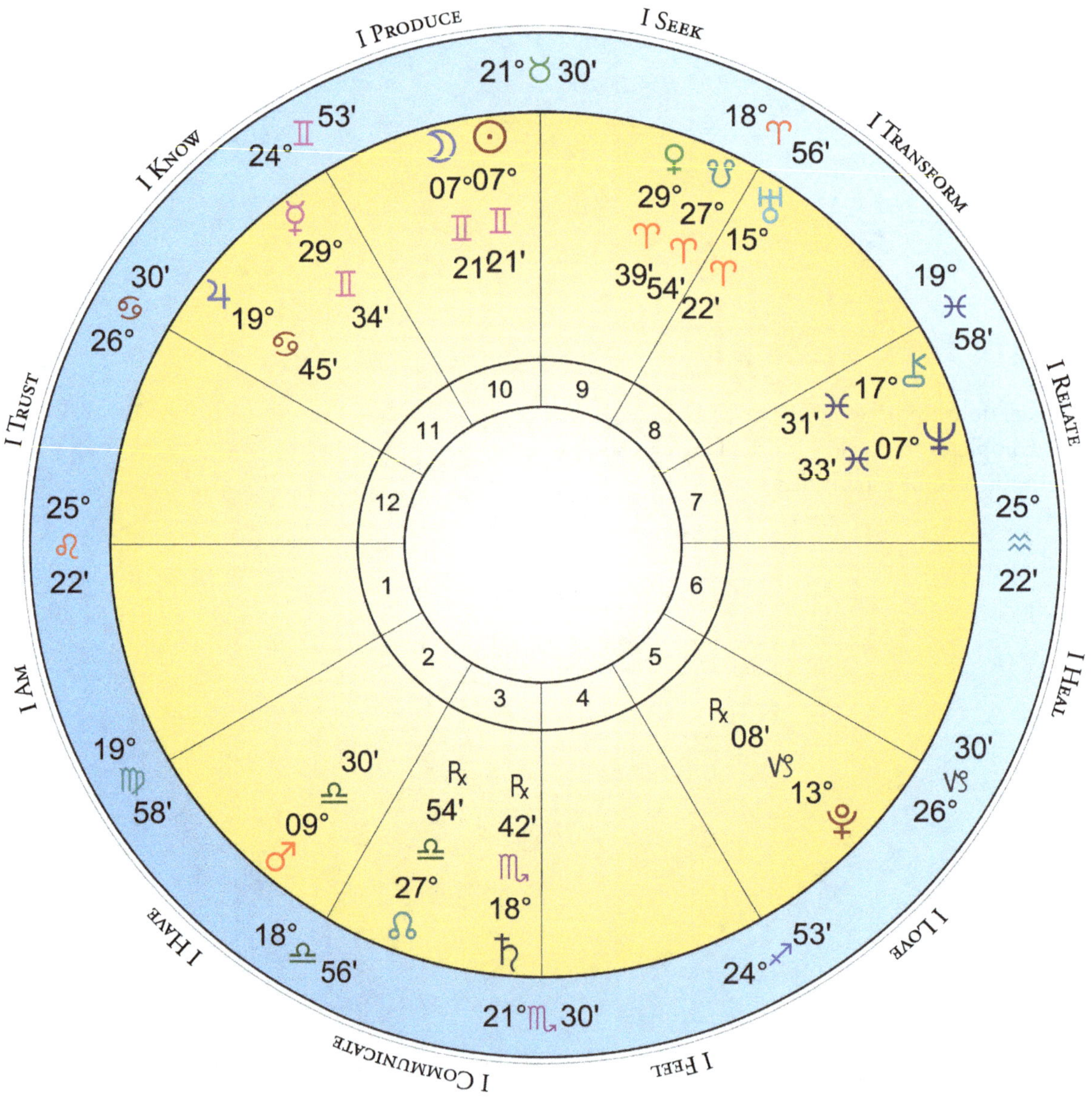

♈ Aries	♋ Cancer	♐ Sagittarius	☽ Moon	♄ Saturn	☊ North Node	V/C Void-of-Course
♉ Taurus	♌ Leo	♑ Capricorn	☿ Mercury	♅ Uranus	☋ South Node	▲ Super-Sensitivity
♊ Gemini	♍ Virgo	♒ Aquarius	♀ Venus	♆ Neptune	➡ Enters	▼ Low-Vitality
	♎ Libra	♓ Pisces	♂ Mars	♇ Pluto	℞ Retrograde	
	♏ Scorpio	☉ Sun	♃ Jupiter	⚷ Chiron	S/D Stationary Direct	

Cosmic Check-In

Take a moment to write a brief phrase for each "I" statement.
This activates all areas of your life for this creative cycle.

♊ I Communicate

♋ I Feel

♌ I Love

♍ I Heal

♎ I Relate

♏ I Transform

♐ I Seek

♑ I Produce

♒ I Know

♓ I Trust

♈ I Am

♉ I Have

June Planetary Highlights

Saturn is Retrograde in Scorpio for the Entire Month

Now is the time to dive into the unknown parts of our inner world. Gather up the emotional courage to do this—it is time to transform our dark, hidden parts into light. Saturn is asking us to strip our fears down to the bone in order to cultivate a true awakening in our consciousness. Pay attention to what you keep avoiding and start there.

Pluto is Retrograde in Capricorn for the Entire Month

This is a time when the core of our existence is looking deep to find a way to be supported. While Pluto is digging deep into the support structures in society, our survival systems want to resist. Trust that, in the digging, Pluto will find the gold mine and bring forth a new and better way for us to feel supported.

June 7 – Mercury goes Retrograde in Cancer

Time to get rid of the clutter in your mind and in your home. Resolve communications with your family and begin to look at family in a new way.

June 9 – Neptune goes Retrograde in Pisces

This is a time to face disappointments—honesty is required here. It is time to take off the rose-colored glasses and ask yourself, "Did my dream not materialize because I didn't give it the right energy, or did I just give up?" Now, take a look and see if you want to re-commit to the idea or if you want to consciously let go of it.

June 12 – Saturn Retrograde in Scorpio Opposes Venus in Taurus

Expect some conflict to show up to make you face reality about being practical. The old man is putting some reigns on your fun. Yuck!!

June 12 – Mars in Libra Opposing Uranus in Aries

Expect a major blast in the relationship area. Recalibrating is necessary right now in order for the new formula for relating to evolve. Question to ask yourself, "How can I be in love and feel free without making a personal war happen?"

June 17 – Mercury Backs into Gemini

This is a brilliant time to check out where you have been misinterpreted. Time to clean this up before moving on.

June 20 – Chiron goes Retrograde in Pisces

Become aware of any pain that is asking for a healing. It's time to connect with old and unnecessary wounds that are in the way of our true expression of joy.

June 21 – Summer Solstice – The Sun Enters Cancer

Look at the garden of life that you have planted so far and see where you need to add fertilizer. Then, pull any weeds that need to come out of your garden.

June 24 – Venus Enters Gemini

Flirting time is here … go for it!

June 27 – The Moon in Cancer Opposing Pluto in Capricorn Retrograde

Romancing the past is in the air during this time, but don't go there. Let your history convert to memory by getting the lesson from the experience and moving on.

Super-Sensitivity – June 6, 7, 12-13 ▲

This is a time when the global atmosphere is sensitive. Expect major changes to happen globally. Be willing to roll with the punches here and work on yourself.

Low-Vitality – June 18-19, 25, and 27 ▼

This is a time when the Earth is low in energy. Know that endings lead to new beginnings. If endings are resisted, progress can't take place and burn-out will happen to you personally. Be willing to allow the Universe to do its work. Let go of needing to know the outcomes.

♈ Aries	♋ Cancer	♐ Sagittarius	☽ Moon	♄ Saturn	☊ North Node	V/C Void-of-Course
♉ Taurus	♌ Leo	♑ Capricorn	☿ Mercury	♅ Uranus	☋ South Node	▲ Super-Sensitivity
♊ Gemini	♍ Virgo	♒ Aquarius	♀ Venus	♆ Neptune	➡ Enters	▼ Low-Vitality
	♎ Libra	♓ Pisces	♂ Mars	♇ Pluto	℞ Retrograde	
	♏ Scorpio	☉ Sun	♃ Jupiter	⚷ Chiron	S/D Stationary Direct	

June

Sunday	Monday	Tuesday	Wednesday	Thursday	Friday	Saturday
1 ♄♇℞ ☽→♌ 6:42PM 9. Reclaim who you are by meditation.	2 ♄♇℞ 10. To move forward, drop the past.	3 ♄♇℞ ☽ V/C 7:41AM 11. Expect powerful magnetics.	4 ♄♇℞ ☽→♍ 7:19AM 3. Choose to see a funny movie.	5 ♄♇℞ 4. Only build on a solid foundation.	6 ♄♇℞ ▲ ☽ V/C 2:12AM ☽→♎ 7:00PM 5. Don't let change upset your plans.	7 ☿♄♇℞ ▲ ☿℞3°♋10′ 4:58AM 6. Honor honesty and integrity.
8 ☿♄♆♇℞ ☽ V/C 12:46PM 7. Know that you know the answer.	9 ☿♄♆♇℞ ♆℞-7°♓35′ 12:52PM ☽→♏ 3:38AM 8. Good leaders can also follow.	10 ☿♄♆♇℞ ☽ V/C 7:20PM 9. Acknowledge the mysteries in life.	11 ☿♄♆♇℞ ☽→♐ 8:23AM 10. Live only in the "now."	12 ☿♄♆♇℞ ▲ ○ 22°♐06′ 9:11 PM ☽ V/C 9:11PM 11. Use your intuition as guidance.	13 ☿♄♆♇℞ ▲ ☽→♑ 10:04AM 3. Find some joy in every day.	14 ☿♄♆♇℞ Flag Day ☽ V/C 11:35PM 4. Dependability creates credibility.
15 ☿♄♆♇℞ Father's Day ☽→♒ 10:27AM 5. Find a different approach.	16 ☿♄♆♇℞ 6. Is your home a reflection of you?	17 ☿♄♆♇℞ ☿℞→♊ 3:06AM ☽ V/C 11:07AM ☽→♓ 11:25AM 7. Trust your inner knowing.	18 ☿♄♆♇℞ ▼ 8.Respect others in your interactions.	19 ☿♄♆♇℞ ▼ ☽ V/C 12:05PM ☽→♈ 2:25PM 9. Be sure to follow your intuition.	20 ☿♄♆⚷♇ ▼ ⚷℞-17°♓46′ 5:45AM 10. Enjoy a new adventure.	21 ☿♄♆⚷♇℞ ☉→♋ 3:52AM Summer Solstice ☽ V/C 3:23PM ☽→♉ 8:03PM 11. Trust your first impression.
22 ☿♄♆⚷♇℞ 3. Your experience creates your belief.	23 ☿♄♆⚷♇℞ ♀→♊ 5:35AM ☽ V/C 6:48PM 4. Use your creative energy for the team.	24 ☿♄♆⚷♇℞ ☽→♊ 4:05AM 5. Allow flexibility in all situations.	25 ☿♄♆⚷♇ ▼ 6. Be honest in serving others.	26 ☿♄♆⚷♇ ▼ ☽ V/C 4:56AM ☽→♋ 2:05PM 7. Be wise in your transactions.	27 ☿♄♆⚷♇ ● 5°♋37′ 1:08 AM 8. Generate abundance.	28 ☿♄♆⚷♇℞ ☽ V/C 6:02PM 9. Pray for truth in all that you do.
29 ☿♄♆⚷♇℞ ☽→♌ 1:42AM 10. A bright future starts in the "now."	30 ☿♄♆⚷♇℞ 2. Know what is right, then decide.					

Full Moon in Sagittarius

June 12, 9:11 PM

The Sun is Opposite the Moon

Full Moons are always in opposition to the Sun. This creates a feeling of tension between where you want to shine and how your feelings are flowing on a sensory level about the Sun's directive. The two forces seem like they are working against each other, yet they are on the same team displaying different techniques to attain the same mission. The Sagittarius/Gemini polarity creates tension between the quest for higher knowledge and the need for academic accolades.

Sagittarius Goddess

Iris, the goddess of the rainbow, is a symbol of multi-colored and multi-dimensional consciousness. She weaves many mysteries into the garment of life with her colors. The Rainbow Bridge gave Iris access to travel between Heaven and Earth. She was Hera's messenger, bringing visions and messages for greater awareness to those who needed insight. For this reason, part of the eye was named after her. The Rainbow is a symbol of a fortunate future and reminds us that we have the potential to manifest in all spheres and circumstances. One of Iris' jobs is to cut the cord of life to those crossing over to the other side and open the directive for the pathway of light. When the Moon is full in Sagittarius, we may find ourselves lost or directionless. It is time to call on the power of Iris to bring a new vision.

On Your Altar

Colors Deep purple, turquoise, royal blue

Numerology 11 – mastering life by paying attention to Universal Law

Tarot Card Temperance – balancing the present with the past, updating yourself

Gemstones Turquoise

Plant remedy Madia – seeing and hitting the target

Fragrance Magnolia – expanded beauty

Degree Choice Points
    22° Sagittarius 05'

Motivation Portals to the new world

Resistance Inflexible tradition

Statement I Seek
   Body Thighs
   Mind Philosophical
   Spirit Inspiration

Element
    Fire – Ability to stand up for yourself, initiates projects, enthusiasm, warmth, gives rise to the expression of the ego.

Twelfth House Moon
    17° Sagittarius 36'

Motivation Child advocacy

Resistance Non-verbal filters

Twelfth House Umbrella Theme
    I Trust – Determines how you deal with your karma, unconscious software, and what you will experience in order to attain mastery by completing your karma. It is also about the way you connect to the Divine.

Meditation

The freedom themes are provided by the zodiac sign and can be from this lifetime or other lifetimes. These meditations assist in dissolving blocks and opening pathways to new frontiers.

When the Moon is in Sagittarius, it is a time to become aware of dependency on rituals and philosophies. Look for perceptions of loyalty, fidelity, and ethics that keep you stuck in the past. Close your eyes and take in a few breaths. Ask for nighttime instructions from the Angel of Records to assist you in discovering a time when you became dependent on a practice that no longer serves you, your truth, your reality, and your daring. The Angel of Ritual will connect you to the new rituals that need to be reawakened at this time to empower your growth in the moment.

Sagittarius Challenges and Victories

Say all of the statements in this section out loud. Then, underline the phrase that means the most to you. Use the phrase as your special affirmation for manifesting and co-creating throughout this phase of the moon.

Today, I blend my old self with my new self, my physical reality with my spiritual awareness, my positive thoughts with my negative thoughts, my past with my present, my feminine with my masculine, my rewards with my losses, my ups with my downs, and my higher self with my lower self. It is a day for me to refine and fine tune my life by looking at my extremes. I recognize what inspires me and what keeps me stuck. I find my center today by acknowledging my extremes. I am aware that balance comes to those who are able to locate the space in the center of these opposite energy fields. When I am in my center my polarities are in motion. Healing cannot occur unless my polarities are moving and I know healing is motion.

I am ready for a healing today and know that by visiting my opposites and determining their vast opposition to each other, I can find the paradoxes that I have chosen for myself and begin to heal. I am willing to experiment with this blending of opposites and become the alchemist of my own life. When I blend all aspects of myself rather than separating them, I can truly become whole. Today is a day to integrate, rather than separate, in order to release the spark of light that stays a prisoner when my polarities are in operation. When I find balance, motion occurs and the Law of Harmony takes over, putting paradoxical energies to rest, thus breaking the crystallization of polarity. The Law of Harmony is beauty in motion, promoting the flow of color, light, sound, and movement into form. Balance is a condition that keeps my spark in motion. I become the vertical line in the center of polarity today and carry the secret of balance. Balance cannot be my goal, motion is my goal today. When I am in motion, I can take action to evolve and to express all of myself freely.

Sagittarius Homework

Time to use your physical body to release the feeling of being caged in by people or circumstances. Choose an activity that burns away confinement and allows you to feel the power of your passion.

The Sagittarius Moon awakens us to know the spark of light that lives in our heart, thus elevating love in ourselves and in our world. This is when we come to realize what is in our highest and best good and we can begin to become free from all that is not lovable in our lives.

Full Moon in Sagittarius

June 12, 9:11 PM

Clearing the Slate for Freedom

Remember a time when you experienced the following trigger points. Write down what happened, forgive yourself, release it, and let it go to clear your slate for freedom.

Unfiltered Language

- Forgive
- Release
- Let go

Bluntness

- Forgive
- Release
- Let go

Exaggerating

- Forgive
- Release
- Let go

Excess

- Forgive
- Release
- Let go

Gambling or Risk-Taking

- Forgive
- Release
- Let go

My Freedom List

Sagittarius Freedom List Ideas

Now is the time to set myself free from belief systems that no longer apply, attitudes that are not uplifting to me, addiction to excess and risk, the need to exaggerate based on low self-esteem, dishonest people, being too blunt, staying in the future and avoiding the NOW, overriding fear by being too optimistic, and preaching.

Full Moon in Sagittarius

June 12, 9:11 PM

How to Use the Moon Book With Your Chart

Fill in the blanks on the Cosmic Check-In page. Then look up the degree of the moon on the chart below. Take note of the "I" statement on the outside of the wheel where the moon is located. Now locate the same degree on your own chart, and make a note of the house and corresponding "I" statement. Go back to the Cosmic Check-In page and circle the two statements from the charts and read what you wrote. This will give you an idea about what to expect from this moon phase on a personal level.

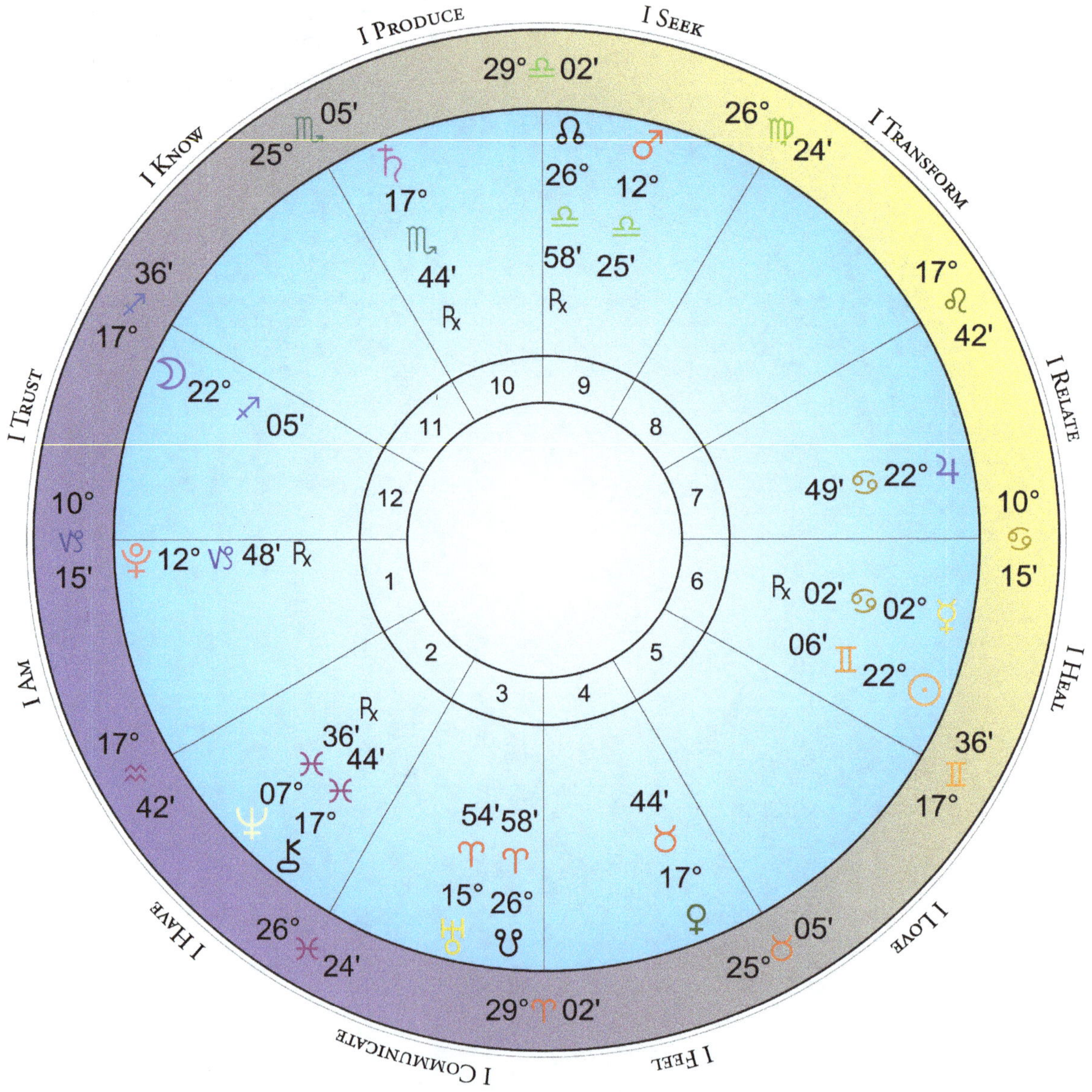

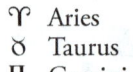

♈ Aries	♋ Cancer	♐ Sagittarius	☽ Moon	♄ Saturn	☊ North Node	V/C Void-of-Course
♉ Taurus	♌ Leo	♑ Capricorn	☿ Mercury	♅ Uranus	☋ South Node	▲ Super-Sensitivity
♊ Gemini	♍ Virgo	♒ Aquarius	♀ Venus	♆ Neptune	➡ Enters	▼ Low-Vitality
	♎ Libra	♓ Pisces	♂ Mars	♇ Pluto	℞ Retrograde	
	♏ Scorpio	☉ Sun	♃ Jupiter	⚷ Chiron	S/D Stationary Direct	

Cosmic Check-In

Take a moment to write a brief phrase for each "I" statement.
This activates all areas of your life for this creative cycle.

♐ I Seek

♑ I Produce

♒ I Know

♓ I Trust

♈ I Am

♉ I Have

♊ I Communicate

♋ I Feel

♌ I Love

♍ I Heal

♎ I Relate

♏ I Transform

New Moon in Cancer

June 27, 1:08 AM

Degree Choice Points
  5° Cancer 37'

Motivation Comfort

Resistance Expendable

Statement I Feel
  Body Breasts
  Mind Nurturing
  Spirit Creator of form

Element
  Water – Divine Feminine, feelings, rhythm, cycles, grace, creativity, receptivity, supporting alignment.

Third House Moon
  16° Gemini 35'

Motivation Refined intellect

Resistance Facing reality

Third House Umbrella Theme
  I Communicate – How you get the word out and the message behind your words.

When the Sun is in Cancer

It is now time to build our structure and foundation. Cancer holds the wisdom of the Great Cosmic Architect. Her statement is, "I build a lighted house and therein I dwell." The key is to use the materials of light, love, and wisdom to build your house and become the creator of form. Look within to see what lights your home and your body. Also check security systems, early environmental training, and mother/child relationships to see what materials you are using to build the structure for your life. Use this creating Moon to build the structure you want.

Cancer Goddess

Birds are the symbol of expanded consciousness because they are born twice; once into the egg and once out of the egg. They are associated with rebirth and self-realization. Bird Woman is the Cancer goddess. She teaches us that, although we live in the illusion that security comes from our identity in the outer world, our true cosmic significance must be found within. Bird Woman directs us toward discovering our way home to our Soul, the place of lotus light. She has the ability to fly between Heaven and Earth, bringing communications from the angels and the spirit guides. She inspires souls to infuse matter with light – the true essence of co-creating.

On Your Altar

Colors Shades of gray, milky/creamy colors

Numerology 8 – expect success

Tarot Card Chariot – the ability to move forward, victory through action

Gemstones Pearl, moonstone, ruby

Plant Remedy Shooting Star – the ability to move straight ahead

Fragrance Peppermint – the essence of the Great Mother

My Co-Creation List

Cancer
Co-Creation Ideas

Now is the time to focus on manifesting being a good mother, new ways to be a mom, nurturing and self-love, the ability to see joy, a clutter-free home, your dream home, and inner and outer security.

This, or something better than this, comes to me in an easy and pleasurable way for the good of all concerned. Thank you, Universe!

New Moon in Cancer

June 27, 1:08 AM

Cancer Challenges and Victories

Say all of the statements in this section out loud. Then, underline the phrase that means the most to you. Use the phrase as your special affirmation for manifesting and co-creating throughout this phase of the moon.

Today I take advantage of my ability to take action and position myself for success. I clearly know that the road to success is before me, and all I need to do is move forward. I am aware that when I take action and move forward, the Universe fills in the dots. Whether I move left or right, or straight ahead doesn't matter—what matters is movement. Today, I release indecisiveness that keeps me stuck. Today, I let go of vacillation that exhausts my mind. Today, I take my foot off of the brakes and find the gas pedal. I allow movement to occur, even if I don't know where I am going. When I take action, I trust the guideposts will appear. I am aware that action leads me to my new direction. So, today I know and GO! I remember that Karma comes to the space of non-action, while success comes through action. Action brings me to my victory. Standing still leads to regret, resentment, and chaos. I am aware that action can be as simple as taking a walk on the beach, buying fresh flowers to add a new dimension to my home, or simply going to a new restaurant for lunch. I take action today to break up a crystallized pattern and, in so doing, my life begins to show me newfound awareness and light to guide me.

Cancer Homework

Cancer co-creates best when catering, writing cookbooks, marriage and family counseling, providing childcare, giving massage, or when engaged in genealogy, arts and crafts, architecture, and home building.

During the Cancer New Moon cycle, we are asked to create light into form and turn it into beauty on four levels. Physically, we must feel nurtured and protected. Emotionally, we must set safe boundaries for the expression of our feelings. Mentally, we must release self-pity and embrace rightful thinking. Spiritually, we must hold the space for the infusion of light to shine inside all bodies on Earth.

Without Acknowledgment Progress Cannot Occur

Acknowledgment creates space for victory and gratitude, which automatically brings us to a level of completion so a new cycle of opportunity can occur in our lives. When we celebrate our wins and acknowledge our victories with gratitude, we update our cells so that our ability to move forward is not hindered by a cellular holographic pattern that is stuck in the past. Cellular lag creates resistance and makes moving forward most difficult. The key is to stay continuously updated by acknowledging yourself for what you did do at the end of each day rather than heading off to sleep thinking about what you did not do. By acknowledging what we didn't do, we play into our karmic storage bank and keep our progress at bay. When we acknowledge ourselves and our manifestations, we are complete, and more cycles of opportunity become available to us in each new day. Be prepared for miracles.

Victory List

Gratitude List

This fulfills the relationship between the giver and the receiver, which completes the cycle with the Universe so that a new beginning can be established.

New Moon in Cancer

June 27, 1:08 AM

How to Use the Moon Book With Your Chart

Fill in the blanks on the Cosmic Check-In page. Then look up the degree of the moon on the chart below. Take note of the "I" statement on the outside of the wheel where the moon is located. Now locate the same degree on your own chart, and make a note of the house and corresponding "I" statement. Go back to the Cosmic Check-In page and circle the two statements from the charts and read what you wrote. This will give you an idea about what to expect from this moon phase on a personal level.

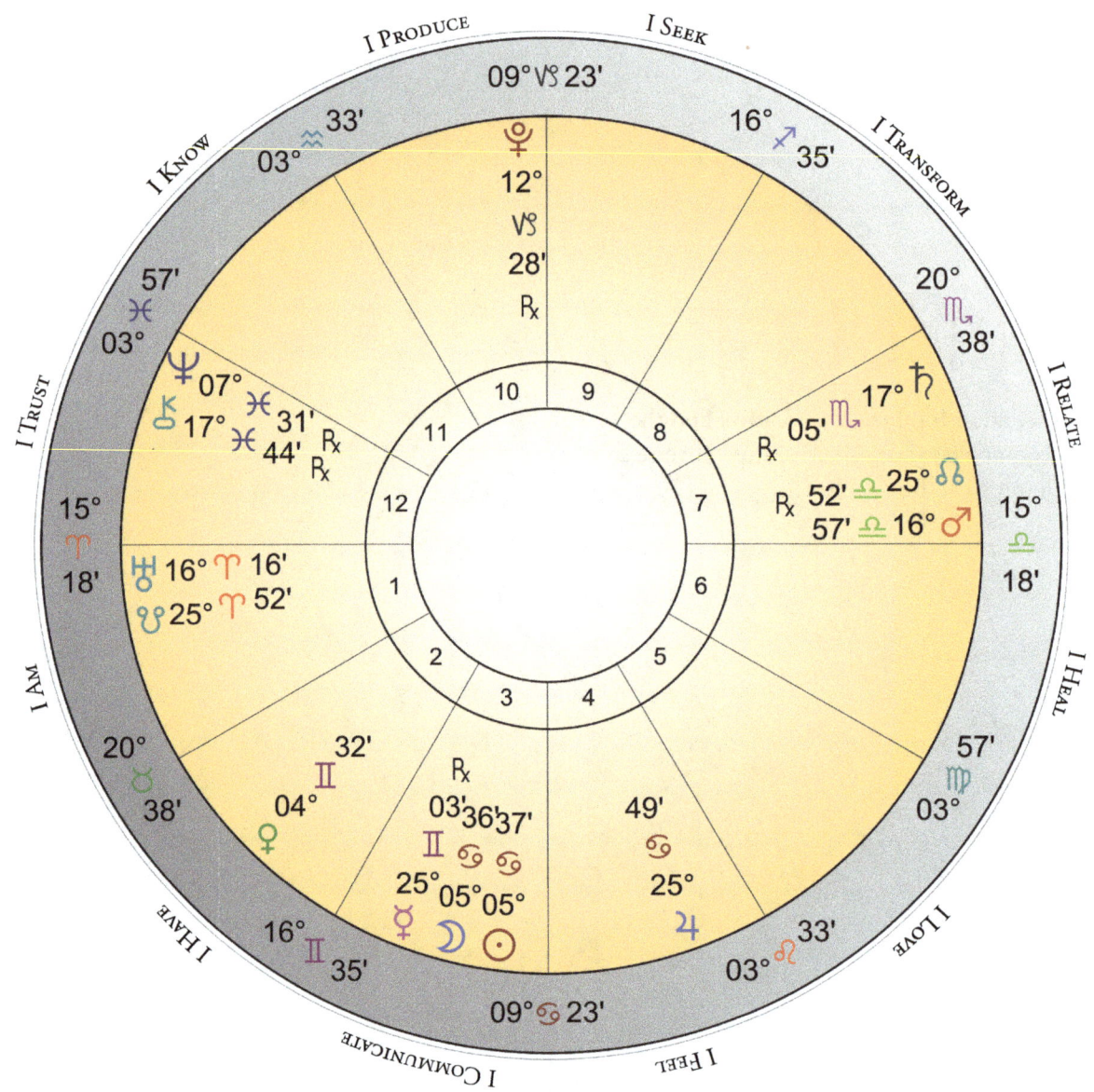

♈ Aries	♋ Cancer	♐ Sagittarius	☽ Moon	♄ Saturn	☊ North Node	V/C Void-of-Course
♉ Taurus	♌ Leo	♑ Capricorn	☿ Mercury	♅ Uranus	☋ South Node	▲ Super-Sensitivity
♊ Gemini	♍ Virgo	♒ Aquarius	♀ Venus	♆ Neptune	➡ Enters	▼ Low-Vitality
	♎ Libra	♓ Pisces	♂ Mars	♇ Pluto	℞ Retrograde	
	♏ Scorpio	☉ Sun	♃ Jupiter	⚷ Chiron	S/D Stationary Direct	

Cosmic Check-In

Take a moment to write a brief phrase for each "I" statement.
This activates all areas of your life for this creative cycle.

♋ I Feel

♌ I Love

♍ I Heal

♎ I Relate

♏ I Transform

♐ I Seek

♑ I Produce

♒ I Know

♓ I Trust

♈ I Am

♉ I Have

♊ I Communicate

125

July Planetary Highlights

Neptune is Retrograde in Pisces for the Entire Month

Try to stay conscious and awake when things get fogged over by the rose-colored glasses. Check in about any addictions that might spring up when emotions are too deep. Awaken to the idea that some of your disappointments might have happened because you gave up. Romancing the idea that you were a victim in any situation is now outdated and does not belong in this time frame.

Chiron is Retrograde in Pisces for the Entire Month

Any flashbacks that arise in your mind are here for a reason. They are signs that something needs to heal inside of you. Act immediately by asking for the wisdom behind the event to come forward so you can heal and bring yourself to the power of the present moment.

Pluto is Retrograde in Capricorn for the Entire Month

It is best to stay away from any fights with government this month. Let Pluto do its own work disabling what doesn't work. Right now we need to stay out of the firing line and avoid a potential landmine—watch, rather than participate.

July 1 – Mercury goes Direct in Gemini

Return to travel plans, open yourself up to the marketplace, and reconcile differences with family and friends where misunderstanding has happened.

Saturn is Retrograde in Scorpio Until July 20

The goal here is to get you free from any indiscretions and untruths you might have hanging around relating to money, sex, power, and death. Take the time to reconcile these issues before the 20th. Remember, we are only as sick as the secrets we keep.

July 21 – Uranus goes Retrograde in Aries

Uranus goes offline and takes a back seat for the next few months. You might want to use this retrograde to bring insight about how you can bring yourself to a state of freedom without rebelling.

July 12 – Mercury Moves into Cancer

Expect the energy to move toward women's issues, home, food, and family. Lots of media will be buzzing about food issues at hand regarding GMOs, organic farming, and healthy eating.

July 16 – Jupiter Moves into Leo

Good fortune now hits show business, art, love affairs, and children. Love is in the air and experiences will be filled with creative expression for the next year. Generosity is all around. Say YES to fun and play!

July 18 – Venus Moves into Cancer

Devote yourself to being nurtured. Take time for many spa days. Work on creative projects that make your heart sing.

July 22 – The Sun Moves into Leo

Yay, it's party time! Have fun in the sun and dance like nobody is watching! The sun is at its highest zenith and activates your creative potential to make sure you allow yourself to fulfill your original intention for being in this lifetime.

July 25 – Mars Moves into Scorpio

Expect your sex drive to be focused. Give yourself a test and learn the difference between sex and sensuality.

July 31 – Mercury Moves into Leo

Expect all communications to spread like wildfire!

Low-Vitality – July 7, 8, 11, 14-17, 22-23 ▼

Be aware that disharmony can really throw you off the beaten path on these days. Stay balanced and know that if you need to rest, do so. The energy is so deep within the Earth right now that there isn't much left for us at this time. Do what your body will allow you to do and don't push your extremes.

Super-Sensitivity – July 9-10 ▲

Slow down to a pace that you can handle to avoid carelessness that could lead to an accident. This is not a good time to travel. The energies in the air are very combustible. Explosions, fire, and thunderstorms are predicted for this time period. These explosions can be personal if you are trying to move energy faster than it can go. Impatience could lead to a disaster.

♈ Aries	♋ Cancer	♐ Sagittarius	☽ Moon	♄ Saturn	☊ North Node	V/C Void-of-Course
♉ Taurus	♌ Leo	♑ Capricorn	☿ Mercury	♅ Uranus	☋ South Node	▲ Super-Sensitivity
♊ Gemini	♍ Virgo	♒ Aquarius	♀ Venus	♆ Neptune	➡ Enters	▼ Low-Vitality
	♎ Libra	♓ Pisces	♂ Mars	♇ Pluto	℞ Retrograde	
	♏ Scorpio	☉ Sun	♃ Jupiter	⚷ Chiron	SD Stationary Direct	

July

Sunday	Monday	Tuesday	Wednesday	Thursday	Friday	Saturday
		1 ♄♆⚷♀℞ ☿SD–24°♊22′ 5:51AM ☽ V/C 2:59AM ☽→♍ 2:23PM 3. Beam joy wherever you go.	2 ♄♆⚷♀℞ 4. Find the structure that works.	3 ♄♆⚷♀℞ ☽ V/C 9:21PM 5. Keep your exercise consistent.	4 ♄♆⚷♀℞ Independence Day ☽→♎ 2:42AM 6. When in doubt, go to your heart.	5 ♄♆⚷♀℞ 7. Find a stimulating new book.
6 ♄♆⚷♀℞ ☽ V/C 8:30AM ☽→♏ 12:33PM 8. Be grateful for all you have.	7 ♄♆⚷♀℞ ▼ 9. Pray for someone in pain.	8 ♄♆⚷♀℞ ▼ ☽ V/C 3:32PM ☽→♐ 6:24PM 10. Take action to fulfill your dreams.	9 ♄♆⚷♀℞ ▲ 2. Act from the point of balance.	10 ♄♆⚷♀ ▲ ☽ V/C 5:19PM ☽→♑ 8:24PM 3. Bring a creative project into form.	11 ♄♆⚷♀ ▼ 4. It works better with a foundation.	12 ♄♆⚷♀℞ ○20°♑03′ 4:24AM ☿→♋ 9:46AM ☽ V/C 6:56PM ☽→♒ 8:06PM 5. Variety makes living enjoyable.
13 ♄♆⚷♀℞ 6. Treat someone to dinner.	14 ♄♆⚷♀ ▼ ☽ V/C 12:22PM ☽→♓ 7:40PM 7. Love exploring the unknown.	15 ♄♆⚷♀ ▼ 8. Your success empowers others.	16 ♄♆⚷♀ ▼ ♃→♌ 4:05AM ☽ V/C 5:57PM ☽→♈ 9:06PM 9. Open up to global awareness.	17 ♄♆⚷♀ ▼ 10. Make a positive contribution.	18 ♄♆⚷♀℞ ♀→♋ 7:07AM ☽ V/C 7:17PM 2. Clarity requires a sense of balance.	19 ♄♆⚷♀℞ ☽→♉ 1:42AM 3. Take time to watch a child play.
20 ♆⚷♀℞ ♄SD 16°♏38′ 1:37PM 4. Erase your limiting patterns.	21 ♅♆⚷♀℞ ♅SR 16°♈30′ 7:54PM ☽ V/C 7:12AM ☽→♊ 9:35AM 5. Enrich you life with travel.	22 ♅♆⚷♀ ▼ ☉→♌ 2:42PM 6. Your smile can make a difference.	23 ♅♆⚷♀ ▼ ☽ V/C 5:52PM ☽→♋ 7:59PM 7. Be clear in your intentions.	24 ♅♆⚷♀℞ 8. Be straight forward, not erratic.	25 ♅♆⚷♀℞ ♂→♏ 7:26PM ☽ V/C 6:53AM 9. Counsel others in a loving manner.	26 ♅♆⚷♀℞ ● 3°♌52′ 3:41PM ☽→♌ 7:54AM 10. Your future is in divine order.
27 ♅♆⚷♀℞ ☽ V/C 5:37PM 2. Going to extremes is futile.	28 ♅♆⚷♀℞ ☽→♍ 8:36PM 3. It's party time! Go out and play.	29 ♅♆⚷♀℞ 4. Keep word and deed in alignment.	30 ♅♆⚷♀℞ 5. Be open to a new direction.	31 ♅♆⚷♀℞ ☿→♌ 3:47PM ☽ V/C 7:47AM ☽→♎ 9:09AM 6. Good health is a blessing.		

Full Moon in Capricorn

July 12, 4:24 AM

The Sun is Opposite the Moon

Full Moons are always in opposition to the Sun. This creates a feeling of tension between where you want to shine and how your feelings are flowing on a sensory level about the Sun's directive. The two forces seem like they are working against each other, yet they are on the same team displaying different techniques to attain the same mission. The Capricorn/Cancer polarity creates tension between the quest for status and the need to feel secure.

Capricorn Goddess

Capricorn goddess, Kali, stands guard with her sword ready to slice away our demons of ignorance and resistance so we can move into our rightful position. She cuts away delusion and denial to assist us in creating beyond the limitations of our mind. Kali reminds us that every experience is an invitation to wake up. She will fight with us every step of the way until we accept our authority with integrity. When we accept her power and embrace Kali, our problems dissolve and we experience radiant bliss, freedom from limitation of the mind, and right use of our power.

On Your Altar

Colors Forest green, earth tones

Numerology 5 – variety, expansion, travel, change

Tarot Card Devil – confinement, attachment to form, look at the broader view

Gemstones Smoky quartz, topaz, garnet

Plant remedy Rosemary – activates appropriate memory

Fragrance Frankincense – assists the Soul's entry into the body

Degree Choice Points
20° Capricorn 02'

Motivation Teamwork

Resistance Undermine

Statement I Produce
Body Knees
Mind Authority issues
Spirit Advance civilization

Element
Earth – Determination, endurance, stability, structure, overly pragmatic, practical, stubborn.

Seventh House Moon
0° Capricorn 16'

Motivation Honor

Resistance Degrades

Seventh House Umbrella Theme
I Relate – One-on-one relationships, defines your people attraction, and how you work in relationships with the people you attract.

Meditation

The freedom themes are provided by the zodiac sign and can be from this lifetime or other lifetimes. These meditations assist in dissolving blocks and opening pathways to new frontiers.

When the Moon is in Capricorn, begin by sitting down in a comfortable position, close your eyes and breathe in and out while asking for the Angel of Humility to show you the kernel of the heart of humility. Begin by releasing arrogance. Review the force of your thrusting will to determine the quality of your executive power. Release irritability and self-reproach. Renew the concept of true devotion and dedicate yourself to the Divine master plan of the Universe. This will set you free.

Capricorn Challenges and Victories

Say all of the statements in this section out loud. Then, underline the phrase that means the most to you. Use the phrase as your special affirmation for manifesting and co-creating throughout this phase of the moon.

I feel limited. I feel confined. I feel stuck. I feel there is no way out. Perhaps I am the target of someone's envy or jealousy, or perhaps I am jealous or I am envious. Maybe I am spending too much time in the outer world and putting too much value on material rewards, things, and possessions. Maybe I am trying to possess someone or limit their view or choice. I may feel there are no choices. Maybe I am living by someone else's rules and beliefs and forgot how to think for myself. I could also be overcome by fear and too terrorized to look at anything at all.

Today, I see and feel the limits of placing the source of love outside myself. I have tunnel vision and I seem to have forgotten to look at my options. I must ask myself today, "How many ways can I look at my life, my situation, or my perceived problems?" Today, I must expand my view to encompass 360° instead of only 180°. I begin by acknowledging to myself that today is the worst it is going to get. I know deep within me that if I allow myself to truly experience my bottom, the top will become visible to me. It is time to look at the brighter side. Begin by identifying the problem by writing it down on a piece of paper. Start with the phrase, "The problem is_____." Fill in the blanks. Then, list as many solutions to the problem as you can. List at least three. Then, say these solutions out loud every day until the answer comes to you through a person, an idea, an event, or a choice.

Capricorn Homework

Put on a good pair of walking shoes and get ready to walk your blues away. It is time to get outside and feel the loving power of mother earth. The green of the trees refreshes your stagnant energy while you exhaust yourself to a point of vulnerability. Then, and only then, will you feel freedom. Give yourself permission to throw your watch away and learn to live in the moment.

The Capricorn moon is the reincarnation of Spirit emerging from the dark waters of our past emotions and releasing us from our fear of change and our fear of loss. Awaken your powerful and positive spiritual connection to be open to new possibilities. Ask yourself to release your emotional loyalty to the past. We are reminded of our need for material and emotional security at this time. In order to ensure this, we must learn to build a foundation for ourselves that is lit from within, made from the materials of love, goodwill, and intelligence.

Full Moon in Capricorn

July 12, 4:24 AM

Clearing the Slate for Freedom

Remember a time when you experienced the following trigger points. Write down what happened, forgive yourself, release it, and let it go to clear your slate for freedom.

Responsibility

- Forgive
- Release
- Let go

Too Much Focus on Work

- Forgive
- Release
- Let go

Too Much Focus on Status and Position

- Forgive
- Release
- Let go

Lacking Compassion

- Forgive
- Release
- Let go

Authority Challenge

- Forgive
- Release
- Let go

My Freedom List

Capricorn
Freedom List Ideas

Now is the time to set myself free from obstacles to success, authority issues, sorrow and sadness, fear that blocks me, arrogance, irritability, limitations of time, priorities that are no longer valid, control and domination, the need to do it all alone, and responsibility.

Full Moon in Capricorn

July 12, 4:24 AM

How to Use the Moon Book With Your Chart

Fill in the blanks on the Cosmic Check-In page. Then look up the degree of the moon on the chart below. Take note of the "I" statement on the outside of the wheel where the moon is located. Now locate the same degree on your own chart, and make a note of the house and corresponding "I" statement. Go back to the Cosmic Check-In page and circle the two statements from the charts and read what you wrote. This will give you an idea about what to expect from this moon phase on a personal level.

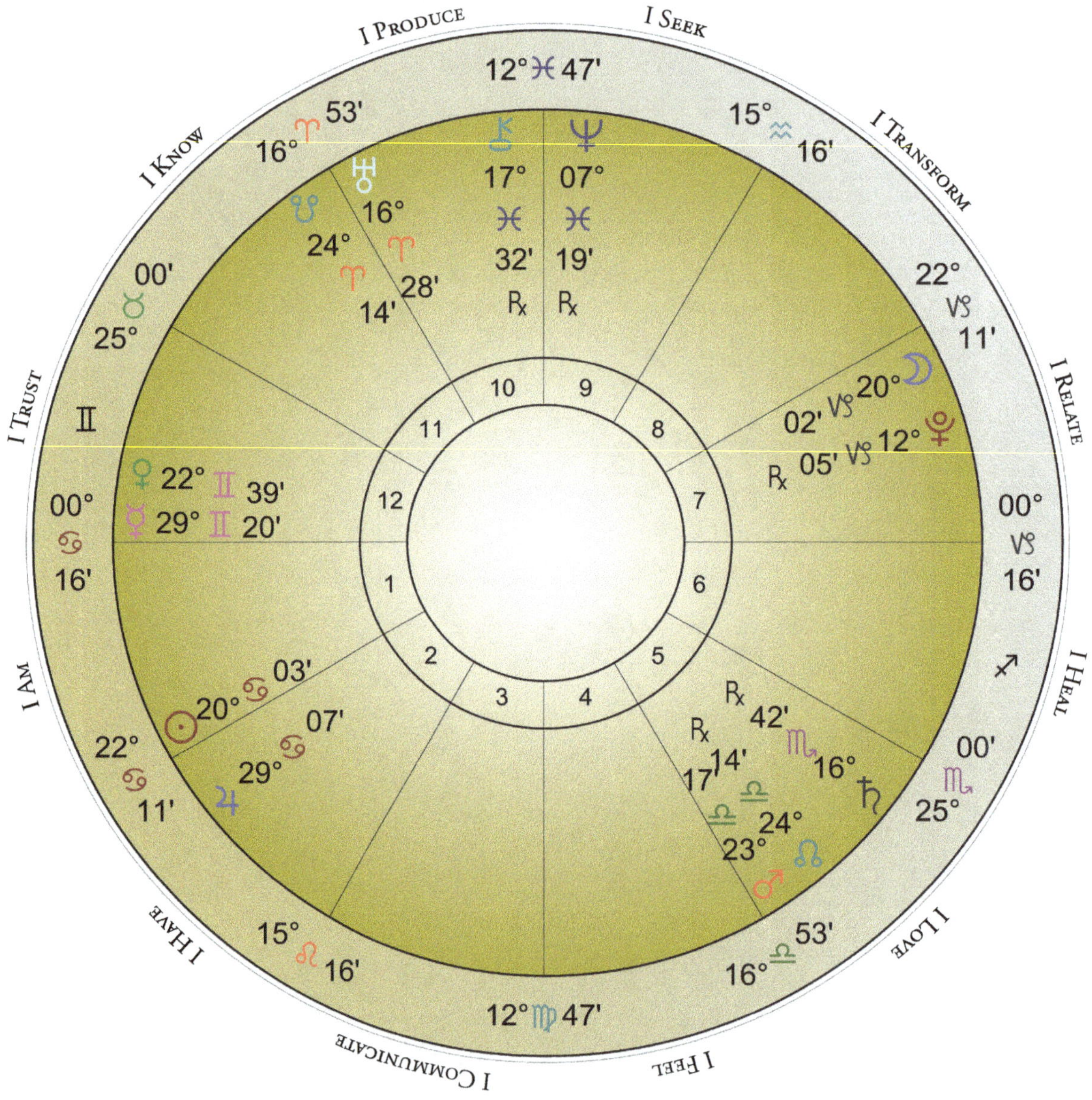

♈ Aries	♋ Cancer	♐ Sagittarius	☽ Moon	♄ Saturn	☊ North Node	V/C Void-of-Course
♉ Taurus	♌ Leo	♑ Capricorn	☿ Mercury	♅ Uranus	☋ South Node	▲ Super-Sensitivity
♊ Gemini	♍ Virgo	♒ Aquarius	♀ Venus	♆ Neptune	➔ Enters	▼ Low-Vitality
	♎ Libra	♓ Pisces	♂ Mars	♇ Pluto	℞ Retrograde	
	♏ Scorpio	☉ Sun	♃ Jupiter	⚷ Chiron	S/D Stationary Direct	

134

Cosmic Check-In

Take a moment to write a brief phrase for each "I" statement.
This activates all areas of your life for this creative cycle.

♑ I Produce

♒ I Know

♓ I Trust

♈ I Am

♉ I Have

♊ I Communicate

♋ I Feel

♌ I Love

♍ I Heal

♎ I Relate

♏ I Transform

♐ I Seek

New Moon in Leo

July 26, 3:41 PM

When the Sun is in Leo

This is the time when we feel the power from the Sun, the heart of the Cosmos. Leo has a direct relationship with the Sun's heart. The Sun rules your identity. Now is the time to shine and stand tall in the center of your life. Allow yourself to feel the power of your individual conscious Self. When we align with the power of the Sun, we become radiant. This radiance gives us the power to transmit energy into life. Personal fulfillment becomes a reality when we align our will with love. Remember to live love every day!

Leo Goddess

The Sun Goddess makes her appearance when the Sun is setting. She paints with the vast pallet of colors available as the day turns to night. She infuses tomorrow's dreams and goals with vitality. She lives in the West where the feminine principle lives. She teaches us to express our creative power potential. She reminds us that the promise of tomorrow comes when we live in truth and integrity and follow the light of our awareness, even through the dark. When the flash of green appears to us at sunset, we know we have connected with the Sun Goddess.

On Your Altar

Colors Royal purple, royal blue, orange

Numerology 10 – your future is here now!

Tarot Card Sun – to stand tall in the center of life

Gemstones Peridot, emerald, amber

Plant Remedy Sunflower – standing tall in the center of your garden

Fragrance Jasmine – remembering your Soul's original intention

Degree Choice Points
 3° Leo 51'

Motivation Prestige

Resistance Overacting

Statement I Love
 Body Heart
 Mind Creativity
 Spirit Good use of will

Element
 Fire – Passion, enthusiasm, warmth, centered in personal identity.

Eighth House Moon
 6° Cancer 22'

Motivation Healing imagination

Resistance Too good to be true

Eighth House Umbrella Theme
 I Transform – How you share money and other resources, what you keep hidden regarding sex, death, money, real estate

My Co-Creation List

Leo Co-Creation Ideas

Now is the time to focus on manifesting new love or new ways of loving, new creative ways of expressing myself, bonding with those I love, quality time with those I love, knowledge of my soul's intention, fun with my children, being a bright beaming light, and connecting to the hearts of humanity.

This, or something better than this, comes to me in an easy and pleasurable way for the good of all concerned. Thank you, Universe!

New Moon in Leo

July 26, 3:41 PM

Leo Challenges and Victories

Say all of the statements in this section out loud. Then, underline the phrase that means the most to you. Use the phrase as your special affirmation for manifesting and co-creating throughout this phase of the moon.

Today, I am at the center of bliss, happiness, abundance, and total celebration. It is my time to shine and feel the power of my true self blasting the Universe, the entire planet, and all of life with the light of my awareness. There is nothing that can stop me today, because I am free to be me. When I am free to be me, I can stand naked in the daylight and have nothing to hide. I truly know that all of life loves me and I love all of life. I feel the radiance and vibration of my being activating me with aliveness, vitality, and charisma. I know that I can make a difference because I celebrate life by infusing, sparking, and igniting matter with light. I am open and ready to embrace all that comes to me with joy. I say "yes!" to all opportunities today; knowing that today is my day. I am in the flow of abundance and I let abundance flow through me.

The child within me is open and ready to play full out; there is not a cloud in the sky today that can eclipse me or place a shadow on me and keep me from my true level of power. I am aware that the child state of being within me simply says yes to action and action is power. When I take action today, my possibilities are endless because they are generated from my true self and motivated by happiness, joy, and freedom. The child within me is able to play full out because I have birthed myself beyond my old perception of blocks. I know that in taking this true power, to be motivated by happiness, pathways on all levels and in all dimensions can open to the empowerment of joy. Empowerment is mine today because I am shining from within myself and I know my deepest self is connected to the source. Empowerment occurs when I live from the inside out. Today, I wave the banner of my being from within, feel the glow, and go.

Leo Homework

The Leo co-creates best through fashion and jewelry design, glamour, politics, super-modeling, movie stardom, child advocacy, fundraising, toy and game design, image consulting, authoring children's books, sales, and cardiology.

Leo gets us closer to our essential self, reminding us of our Soul's original intention. We become ready to receive the benefits of reflective light and radiating light at the same time so that we can see our personality and our soul connecting to love which constitutes a new level of fulfillment. Expect purification, transmutation, communication, and mastery to be part of your personal experience.

Without Acknowledgment Progress Cannot Occur

Acknowledgment creates space for victory and gratitude, which automatically brings us to a level of completion so a new cycle of opportunity can occur in our lives. When we celebrate our wins and acknowledge our victories with gratitude, we update our cells so that our ability to move forward is not hindered by a cellular holographic pattern that is stuck in the past. Cellular lag creates resistance and makes moving forward most difficult. The key is to stay continuously updated by acknowledging yourself for what you did do at the end of each day rather than heading off to sleep thinking about what you did not do. By acknowledging what we didn't do, we play into our karmic storage bank and keep our progress at bay. When we acknowledge ourselves and our manifestations, we are complete, and more cycles of opportunity become available to us in each new day. Be prepared for miracles.

Victory List

Gratitude List

This fulfills the relationship between the giver and the receiver, which completes the cycle with the Universe so that a new beginning can be established.

New Moon in Leo

July 26, 3:41 PM

How to Use the Moon Book With Your Chart

Fill in the blanks on the Cosmic Check-In page. Then look up the degree of the moon on the chart below. Take note of the "I" statement on the outside of the wheel where the moon is located. Now locate the same degree on your own chart, and make a note of the house and corresponding "I" statement. Go back to the Cosmic Check-In page and circle the two statements from the charts and read what you wrote. This will give you an idea about what to expect from this moon phase on a personal level.

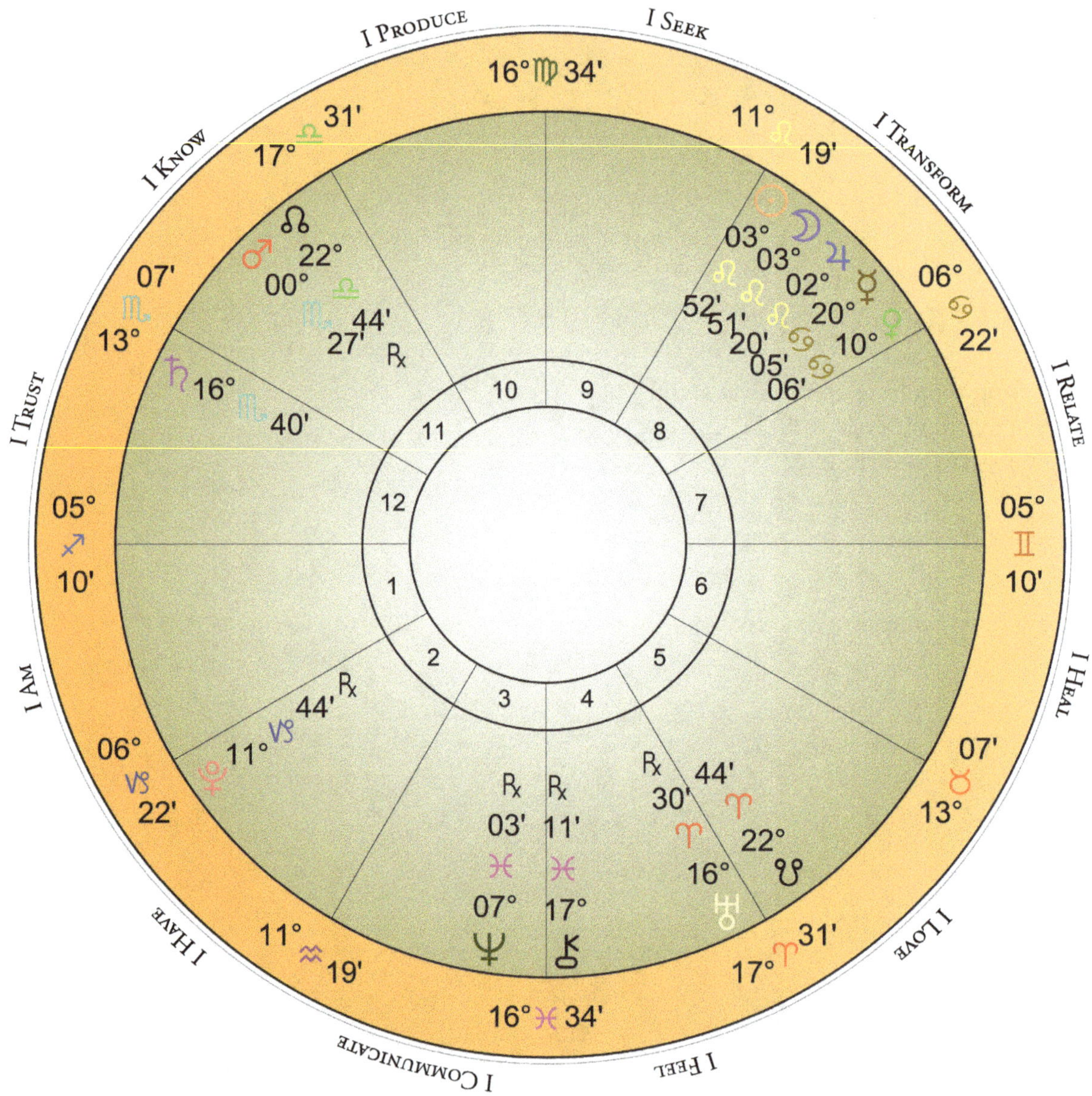

♈ Aries	♋ Cancer	♐ Sagittarius	☽ Moon	♄ Saturn	☊ North Node	V/C Void-of-Course
♉ Taurus	♌ Leo	♑ Capricorn	☿ Mercury	♅ Uranus	☋ South Node	▲ Super-Sensitivity
♊ Gemini	♍ Virgo	♒ Aquarius	♀ Venus	♆ Neptune	➡ Enters	▼ Low-Vitality
	♎ Libra	♓ Pisces	♂ Mars	♇ Pluto	℞ Retrograde	
	♏ Scorpio		☉ Sun	⚷ Chiron	S/D Stationary Direct	

Cosmic Check-In

Take a moment to write a brief phrase for each "I" statement.
This activates all areas of your life for this creative cycle.

♌ I Love

♍ I Heal

♎ I Relate

♏ I Transform

♐ I Seek

♑ I Produce

♒ I Know

♓ I Trust

♈ I Am

♉ I Have

♊ I Communicate

♋ I Feel

August Planetary Highlights

Uranus is Retrograde in Aries for the Entire Month

This will give us time to understand how important it is for us to revamp our personality, so that it can take on a new point of reference without impulsive action.

Neptune is Retrograde in Pisces for the Entire Month

Expect your senses to be heightened and your perception to become more acute. This is a time when we're able to see what really exists instead of what we wish existed. Time to get your head out of the clouds and make some new choices with your feet on the ground.

Chiron is Retrograde in Pisces for the Entire Month

Do not neglect yourself—it is time to heal.

Pluto is Retrograde in Capricorn for the Entire Month

Expect systems to move into a transformational process, especially related to business. What used to feel grounded and structured will feel a bit shaky during this month. The business paradigm is going to be revamped. Your survival issues may come up, depending on how dependent you are on structure and systems. Take this time to review and allow yourself to be open to new ways to approach the systems that are present in your life, so that the transformation can occur without the stress of resistance.

August 10 – The Sun and Mercury Dance Together in Leo

This is a time to speak about the radiance that you feel in your heart without letting your logic get in the way. Write a love letter.

August 12 – Venus Enters Leo

Take time out to play and remember that life is a celebration, even in the midst of change. Make sure to go shopping and have a party to open your heart to love.

August 15 – Mercury Enters Virgo

Details can become overwhelming if you let them take over your mind. Find Divinity in the details and let your mind celebrate the discovery.

August 22 – The Sun Enters Virgo

It is healing time. Take time to study herbs, gardening, and what it takes to be a good steward to Mother Earth. Small spaces come forward to be dealt with now, so set good boundaries and make yourself comfortable inside your body.

August 26 – Mars and Saturn are Coupled in Scorpio

This coupling could create a feeling of confinement. If you try to push, it will backfire. Take action to go deep down inside your dark side to see what needs to recalibrate. Don't worry, Saturn will gladly show you what needs improvement by creating triggers for you.

Super-Sensitivity – August 6-7 ▲

Be careful. Reaction, retaliation, and criticism (of self or others) is in the air at this time. It is best to stay within your own process. Release the need for approval or advice from others, since it could lead to defensive behaviors that you will regret later.

Low-Vitality – August 19-20 ▼

Beware of burnout on these days. This pattern promotes exhaustion that could have an effect on the body if you don't take time out to rest when you are tired. Do what it takes to monitor yourself, and change your plans if you feel out of balance. Revitalize with breath work and meditation. Do whatever it takes to relax and get centered in this hyperactive energy field. If you meet with resistance, back off and let go.

Remember, power is no longer in style. Empowerment is where it is all happening and is far less exhausting.

♈ Aries	♋ Cancer	♐ Sagittarius	☽ Moon	♄ Saturn	☊ North Node	V/C Void-of-Course
♉ Taurus	♌ Leo	♑ Capricorn	☿ Mercury	♅ Uranus	☋ South Node	▲ Super-Sensitivity
♊ Gemini	♍ Virgo	♒ Aquarius	♀ Venus	♆ Neptune	➡ Enters	▼ Low-Vitality
	♎ Libra	♓ Pisces	♂ Mars	♇ Pluto	℞ Retrograde	
	♏ Scorpio		☉ Sun	♃ Jupiter	⚷ Chiron	S/D Stationary Direct

August

Sunday	Monday	Tuesday	Wednesday	Thursday	Friday	Saturday
					1 ♅♆⚷♇℞ ☽ V/C 7:57PM 7. Master creative, intuitive thinking.	2 ♅♆⚷♇℞ ☽→♏ 7:56PM 8. Put action into your commitment.
3 ♅♆⚷♇℞ 9. Honor your feelings today.	4 ♅♆⚷♇℞ ☽ V/C 10:42AM 10. Travel helps broaden the mind.	5 ♅♆⚷♇℞ ☽→♐ 3:18AM 2. When in doubt, check it out.	6 ♅♆⚷♇℞ ▲ ☽ V/C 7:51AM 3. Take action with your ideas.	7 ♅♆⚷♇℞ ▲ ☽→♑ 6:38AM 4. Loyalty is a badge of honor.	8 ♅♆⚷♇℞ 6. Heartfelt love is unconditional.	9 ♅♆⚷♇℞ ☽ V/C 1:08AM ☽→♒ 6:51AM 7. Positive mind, positive influence.
10 ♅♆⚷♇℞ ○ 18°♒2' 11:09 AM ☽ V/C 3:11PM 8. Remember, as above, so below.	11 ♅♆⚷♇℞ ☽→♓ 5:55AM 9. The power of prayer is awesome.	12 ♅♆⚷♇℞ ☽ V/C 9:00AM ♀→♌ 12:25AM 10. A fresh start works wonders.	13 ♅♆⚷♇℞ ☽→♈ 6:00AM 2. Reassess priorities, then act.	14 ♅♆⚷♇℞ 3. Shed old beliefs to open joy.	15 ♅♆⚷♇℞ ☽ V/C 8:50AM ☽→♉ 8:57AM ☿→♍ 9:45AM 4. Stand strong in what you know.	16 ♅♆⚷♇℞ 5. Set a steady pace for yourself.
17 ♅♆⚷♇℞ ☽ V/C 5:25AM ☽→♊ 3:41PM 6. Let your heart direct you.	18 ♅♆⚷♇℞ 7. Do research on an intriguing idea.	19 ♅♆⚷♇ ▼ ☽ V/C 7:53PM 8.Limited thinking blocks manifesting.	20 ♅♆⚷♇ ▼ ☽→♋ 1:44AM 9. Communicate your feelings.	21 ♅♆⚷♇℞ ☽ V/C 12:33PM 10. Replace the old with innovation.	22 ♅♆⚷♇℞ ☽→♌ 1:49PM ☉→♍ 9:47PM 2. Balance leads to adaptability.	23 ♅♆⚷♇℞ 3. Bring your joy to your friends.
24 ♅♆⚷♇℞ ☽ V/C 1:25AM 4. Follow the plan that's best for you.	25 ♅♆⚷♇℞ ● 2°♍19' 7:12 AM ☽→♍ 2:32AM 5. New directions add variety.	26 ♅♆⚷♇℞ ☽ V/C 7:28PM 6. All we are is love.	27 ♅♆⚷♇℞ ☽→♎ 2:54PM 7. Radical thinking works best.	28 ♅♆⚷♇℞ 8. Good team players succeed.	29 ♅♆⚷♇℞ ☽ V/C 8:59AM 9. Live in the center of your prayer.	30 ♅♆⚷♇℞ ☽→♏ 1:52AM 10. Half the fun is creating the plan.
31 ♅♆⚷♇℞ 2. Gather facts, then decide.						

Full Moon in Aquarius

August 10, 11:09 AM

Degree Choice Points
  18° Aquarius 02'

Motivation Calm after the storm

Resistance Fear of experience

Statement I Know
  Body Ankles
  Mind Abandonment issues
  Spirit Vision

Element
  Air – Directs consciousness towards form through curiosity, learning, and flexibility.

Fourth House Moon
  22° Capricorn 27'

Motivation Acknowledgment

Resistance Criticism

Fourth House Umbrella Theme
  I Feel – The way your early environmental training was, how that set your foundation for living, and why you chose your mother.

The Sun is Opposite the Moon

Full Moons are always in opposition to the Sun. This creates a feeling of tension between where you want to shine and how your feelings are flowing on a sensory level about the Sun's directive. The two forces seem like they are working against each other, yet they are on the same team displaying different techniques to attain the same mission. The Aquarius/Leo polarity creates tension between the quest for group interaction and recognition of self.

Aquarius Goddess

Hera, the Queen of Heaven, was responsible for every aspect of existence. Her name means "Great Lady." Legend has it that she created the Milky Way from the milk in her breasts. When the drops of milk came to Earth, white lily fields manifested everywhere. Hera was the only goddess who accompanied women through every aspect of their lives. She was the great protector of their marriages, their children, and their welfare. She was an advocate for women until she married Zeus and had a complete personality change, cursing all women in whom Zeus was interested sexually. Scorned, she turned vindictive toward the women who were the objects of Zeus' desire, rather that placing her rage on Zeus, where it belonged. Her jealously became her trademark. When the Moon is full in Aquarius we must learn the Art of Detachment so we don't sell out to emotional entrapments.

On Your Altar

Colors Electric colors, neon, multi-colors, pearl white

Numerology 8 – manifest success in all areas of your life today

Tarot Card Star – being guided by a higher source

Gemstones Aquamarine, amethyst, opal

Plant remedy Queen of the Night Cactus – the ability to see in the dark

Fragrance Myrrh – healing the nervous system

Meditation

The freedom themes are provided by the zodiac sign and can be from this lifetime or other lifetimes. These meditations assist in dissolving blocks and opening pathways to new frontiers.

The Aquarius Full Moon promotes the rearrangement of plans. Sit quietly and close your eyes, breathe in and breathe out while watching for sudden changes in priorities and an urge to express yourself more freely. Watch out for hyperactivity and carelessness. The unexpected breakthrough in an ungratifying situation can occur, sparking the creation of a new pathway. Take time to connect to angelic forces to see the other side of frenzy and fantasy in order to know practical passion. Reconcile with times when your zeal has hurt others. Make contact with the magnetic energy currents of the atmosphere to recharge the body and behold the cosmic braille points of things to come. Receive instructions from the higher worlds to be the guardian of the unknown inventive treasures.

Aquarius Challenges and Victories

Say all of the statements in this section out loud. Then, underline the phrase that means the most to you. Use the phrase as your special affirmation for manifesting and co-creating throughout this phase of the moon.

Today my true potential can be realized. All I have to do is take a risk and know that my faith is in operation. My future is very bright and offers me a promise of things to come. Today is a day of destiny. I have chosen this day to determine a DESTINY PROMISE I MADE TO MYSELF BEFORE I CAME INTO THIS LIFE. All that is required of me is to move out of my comfort zone and take a risk. I am aware that faith cannot be determined without risk. I take the risk to move into the next space of creation in my life. I release fear and move into faith, knowing full well that my logic and reason are part of the fear that keeps me stuck.

I am reminded that the kingdom of heaven is open to the child. I find the child within me today to embrace what life has for me with open arms and a spirit of adventure. I know my true potential lives inside my magical child and she/he is willing to play and go for the gusto. I am here in this life to fulfill my promise to experience life to the fullest and to release the fear of judgment that has hounded me and kept me from playing full-out. I remember that when I experience, I gather a knowledge base within my Soul and keep my agreement with myself and the Universe. I connect to my super-consciousness and take on the bigger view of my life and all that it has to offer me when I risk reason and take a leap of faith. I know in the depth of my awareness that, if I jump off the diving board, there will be water in the pool. I am willing to risk reason for an experience. Everything I ever wanted is one step outside my comfort zone. I go for the GUSTO today! I release my fear today and turn it into faith. I trust in the promise of things to come. I know my potential is realized today, and that all I have to do is say "yes!" to life!

Aquarian Homework

The Aquarius moon reminds us of our connection to solar fire (the heart of the Sun) also known as the Heart of the Cosmos. During this time, we get our vitality recharged and our potent power comes into play motivating the masses to receive more energy to transmute into the new world. Voice all that you know to be true to the point of self-realization where your authentic purpose can be revealed to you. This is the moment where you have released all that has kept you from your true sense of freedom. Remember to replenish all the electrolytes in your system.

Full Moon in Aquarius

August 10, 11:09 AM

Clearing the Slate for Freedom

Remember a time when you experienced the following trigger points. Write down what happened, forgive yourself, release it, and let it go to clear your slate for freedom.

Stubborn

- Forgive
- Release
- Let go

Spiritual Elitism

- Forgive
- Release
- Let go

Frenzy and Chaos

- Forgive
- Release
- Let go

Living in the Future

- Forgive
- Release
- Let go

Rebellion

- Forgive
- Release
- Let go

My Freedom List

Aquarius Freedom List Ideas
Now is the time to set myself free from resistance to authority figures, blocks to living in the moment, unnecessary rebellion, non-productive frenzy and fantasy, the need to be spontaneous, and people who aren't team players.

Full Moon in Aquarius

August 10, 11:09 AM

How to Use the Moon Book With Your Chart

Fill in the blanks on the Cosmic Check-In page. Then look up the degree of the moon on the chart below. Take note of the "I" statement on the outside of the wheel where the moon is located. Now locate the same degree on your own chart, and make a note of the house and corresponding "I" statement. Go back to the Cosmic Check-In page and circle the two statements from the charts and read what you wrote. This will give you an idea about what to expect from this moon phase on a personal level.

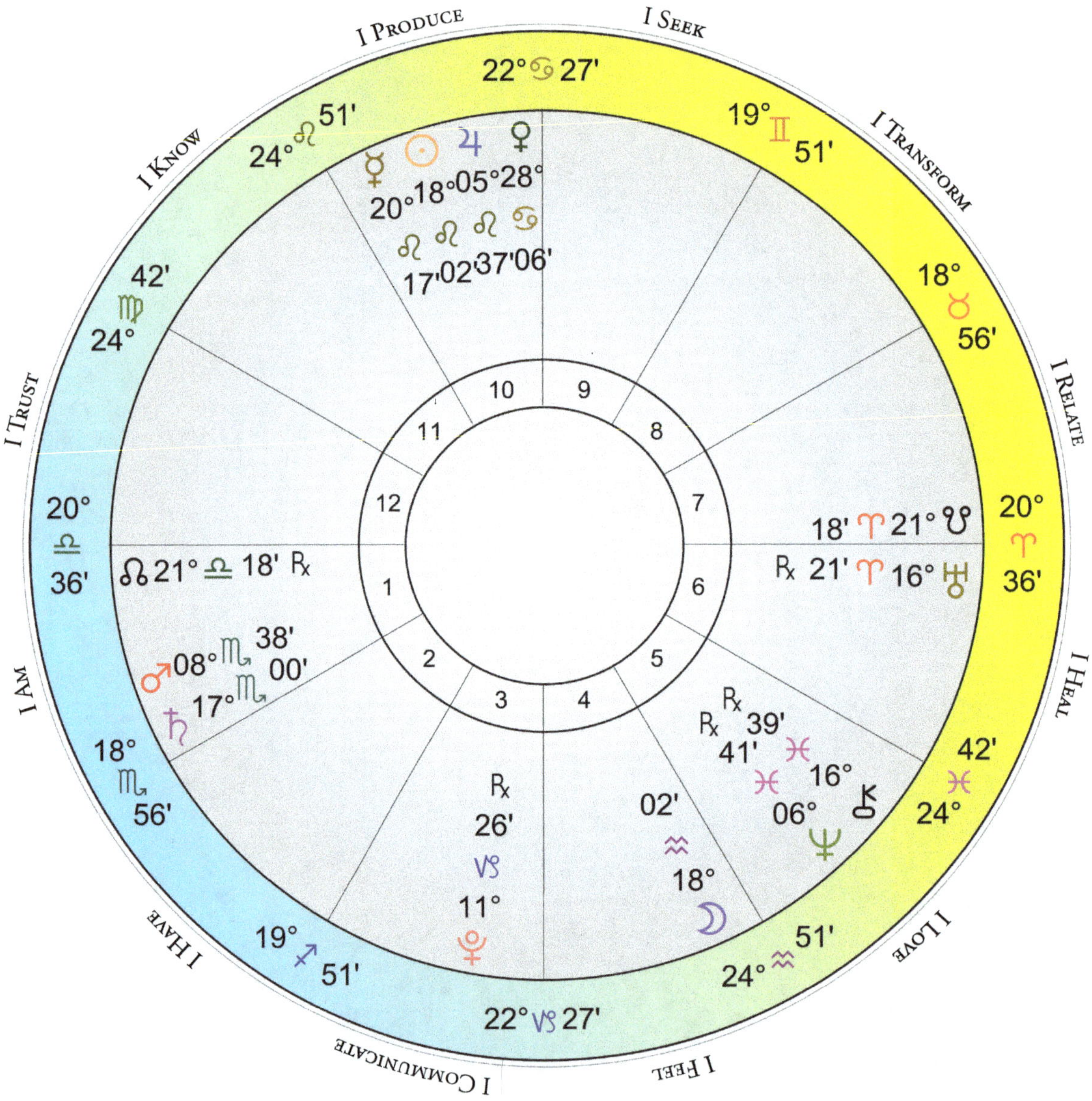

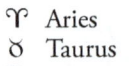

♈ Aries	♋ Cancer	♐ Sagittarius	☽ Moon	♄ Saturn	☊ North Node	V/C Void-of-Course
♉ Taurus	♌ Leo	♑ Capricorn	☿ Mercury	♅ Uranus	☋ South Node	▲ Super-Sensitivity
♊ Gemini	♍ Virgo	♒ Aquarius	♀ Venus	♆ Neptune	➡ Enters	▼ Low-Vitality
	♎ Libra	♓ Pisces	♂ Mars	♇ Pluto	℞ Retrograde	
	♏ Scorpio	☉ Sun	♃ Jupiter	⚷ Chiron	S/D Stationary Direct	

152

Cosmic Check-In

Take a moment to write a brief phrase for each "I" statement.
This activates all areas of your life for this creative cycle.

♒ I Know

♓ I Trust

♈ I Am

♉ I Have

♊ I Communicate

♋ I Feel

♌ I Love

♍ I Heal

♎ I Relate

♏ I Transform

♐ I Seek

♑ I Produce

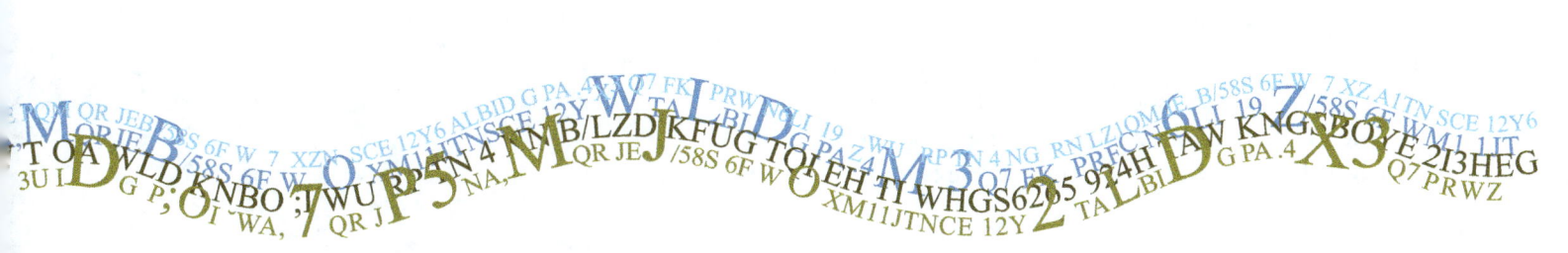

New Moon in Virgo

August 25, 7:12 AM

When the Sun is in Virgo

Virgo is called the "Womb of Time" in which the seeds of great value are planted, shielded, nourished, and revealed. It is the labor of Virgo that brings the Christ Principle into manifestation within individuals and mankind. This unification occurs when we feel the power within us to serve. When we serve, we give birth to Divinity. Virgo time is when we all have a chance to raise the standard of excellence in our lives and on the Earth. The Virgo intelligence stores and maintains light in a precise manner. Attention to detail is Virgo's great gift to life.

Virgo Goddess

The Virgo goddess, Cosmic Womb Woman, gives birth to Divinity. She is a symbol of the ability to give birth to the Self in order to serve, perfect, and purify. It is Cosmic Womb Woman who urges each human to fulfill the goal of evolution by planting seeds of love and power, sending the spark of light to each atom, plant, animal, and planet in the entire solar system.

On Your Altar

Colors Earth tones, blue, green

Numerology 5 – action is now…Know and Go!

Tarot Card The Hermit – being a shining light for all of life

Gemstones Emerald, malachite, sapphire

Plant Remedy Sagebrush – the ability to hold and store light

Fragrance Lavender – management and storage of energy

Degree Choice Points
   2° Virgo 18'

Motivation Assisted turning points

Resistance Aloofness

Statement I Heal
   Body Intestines
   Mind Critical
   Spirit Divinity in the details

Element
   Earth – Family lineage and DNA healing, healing power from the plant kingdom, knowing nutrition and abundance, body awareness, connection to small animals.

Twelfth House Moon
   14° Leo 27'

Motivation Shows solidarity

Resistance Disruptions

Twelfth House Umbrella Theme
   I Trust – Determines how you deal with your karma, unconscious software, and what you will experience in order to attain mastery by completing your karma. It is also about the way you connect to the Divine.

My Co-Creation List

Virgo Co-Creation Ideas

Now is the time to focus on manifesting a high standard of excellence, a healthy lifestyle, self-acceptance, discernment without judgment, healing abilities, contribution to Nature, and a healthy body.

This, or something better than this, comes to me in an easy and pleasurable way for the good of all concerned. Thank you, Universe!

New Moon in Virgo

August 25, 7:12 AM

Virgo Challenges and Victories

Say all of the statements in this section out loud. Then, underline the phrase that means the most to you. Use the phrase as your special affirmation for manifesting and co-creating throughout this phase of the moon.

Today, I recognize what I love most about myself. I am the source of my love, my life, and my experience. I will set aside time today to nurture myself. I allow myself to receive these gifts and know in my heart that it is natural for me to love myself. I discover, deep within myself, the knowing that the love I give myself is commensurate to the love I am willing to receive from others. I am aware that what I expect from others cannot be truly expressed or experienced if I cannot give to myself first. I can never be disappointed when I know that love is a natural resource for me today.

Today, I honor the Earth by acknowledging what she has given me. I take time out to walk in the woods or on the beach, to feel the power of the creative pulse of the creative forces flowing through my body with the energy of being alive. I spend time in my garden and plant flowers to enhance the idea of beauty today. I honor my body today and get a massage. I spend quality time sharing joyful moments with those who love to connect from the heart and realize the blessings that come from living my life with love.

Virgo Homework

Virgo co-creates best through working with herbology, folk medicine, environmental industries, organic farming, recycling, horticulture, acupuncture, healing arts, nutritional counseling, yoga instruction, and editing.

The Virgo moon cycle gives birth to Divinity in its own unique way, understanding the Soul's blueprint to be a temple of beauty. This creates what is known as the "crisis of perfection" within the minds of mankind during this time. We become aware of Spirit ascending and descending at the same time and must recognize that these contradicting energies are working within us in order to give birth to Divinity.

Without Acknowledgment Progress Cannot Occur

Acknowledgment creates space for victory and gratitude, which automatically brings us to a level of completion so a new cycle of opportunity can occur in our lives. When we celebrate our wins and acknowledge our victories with gratitude, we update our cells so that our ability to move forward is not hindered by a cellular holographic pattern that is stuck in the past. Cellular lag creates resistance and makes moving forward most difficult. The key is to stay continuously updated by acknowledging yourself for what you did do at the end of each day rather than heading off to sleep thinking about what you did not do. By acknowledging what we didn't do, we play into our karmic storage bank and keep our progress at bay. When we acknowledge ourselves and our manifestations, we are complete, and more cycles of opportunity become available to us in each new day. Be prepared for miracles.

Victory List

Gratitude List

This fulfills the relationship between the giver and the receiver, which completes the cycle with the Universe so that a new beginning can be established.

New Moon in Virgo

August 25, 7:12 AM

How to Use the Moon Book With Your Chart

Fill in the blanks on the Cosmic Check-In page. Then look up the degree of the moon on the chart below. Take note of the "I" statement on the outside of the wheel where the moon is located. Now locate the same degree on your own chart, and make a note of the house and corresponding "I" statement. Go back to the Cosmic Check-In page and circle the two statements from the charts and read what you wrote. This will give you an idea about what to expect from this moon phase on a personal level.

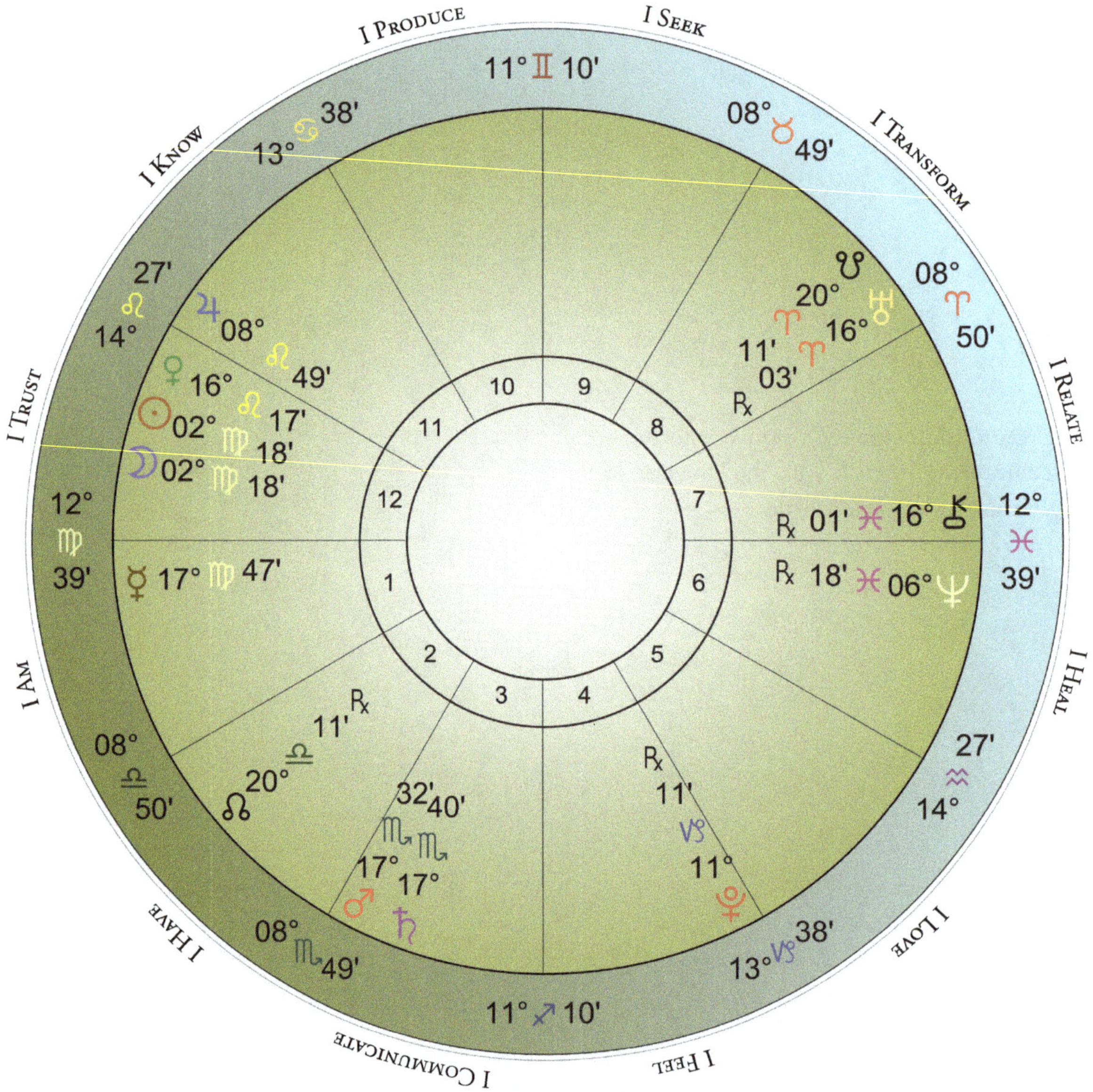

♈ Aries	♋ Cancer	♐ Sagittarius	☽ Moon	♄ Saturn	☊ North Node	V/C Void-of-Course
♉ Taurus	♌ Leo	♑ Capricorn	☿ Mercury	⛢ Uranus	☋ South Node	▲ Super-Sensitivity
♊ Gemini	♍ Virgo	♒ Aquarius	♀ Venus	♆ Neptune	➡ Enters	▼ Low-Vitality
	♎ Libra	♓ Pisces	♂ Mars	♇ Pluto	℞ Retrograde	
	♏ Scorpio	☉ Sun	♃ Jupiter	⚷ Chiron	SD Stationary Direct	

Cosmic Check-In

Take a moment to write a brief phrase for each "I" statement.
This activates all areas of your life for this creative cycle.

♍ I Heal

♎ I Relate

♏ I Transform

♐ I Seek

♑ I Produce

♒ I Know

♓ I Trust

♈ I Am

♉ I Have

♊ I Communicate

♋ I Feel

♌ I Love

September Planetary Highlights

Uranus is Retrograde in Aries for the Entire Month

This promotes a need to pursue inner freedom, and having to face all of the frustration that arises when the higher ideal of inner freedom becomes challenged by the tribal attitudes of the past. Expect your new ideals to be challenged. Watch out for rebellion.

Neptune is Retrograde in Pisces for the Entire Month

This stimulates the desire to create the ideal society and there is a sense of disappointment because that actualization has not happened yet. Now is the time to take a stand and join a group or create a group that can assist people in being connected to the ideas of peace and love.

Chiron is Retrograde in Pisces for the Entire Month

This is a chance to expose and clarify hidden areas where you feel "less than," and heal them. This will be especially appropriate if you've been denying or avoiding the discomfort.

Pluto is Retrograde Until Sept. 22

This is a time to become aware of our reluctance to change, to transform, to expand, and to accept what life requires. There are survival issues connected with any group or set of morals, customs, traditions, or religious beliefs. Become aware of those you are hanging onto at this time and know they will be challenged. See where you are avoiding your truth and clinging to a thread of someone else's truth in order to survive. Look beneath the surface to determine your own truth and be willing to look deep within to find it. Notice where you feel uncomfortable, and take the dive to discover what you already know and have been hiding from yourself.

September 1 – Mercury Moves into Libra

The windshield wipers of the mind become very active in this area. Watch your mind and avoid vacillation and indecisiveness. Remember, if you can't make a decision within 3 minutes, it is not the right time. The "Know and Go" theme for this year will come in handy during this time.

September 5 – Venus Moves into Virgo

Divinity is in the details here. There is a tendency to become overly-interested in the way you look. Take time out to use your creative nature to raise the standard of excellence in something bigger than yourself.

September 13 – Mars Moves into Sagittarius

Freedom becomes a major issue right now. The need to travel to distant places is in the forefront of your experience. Go for it and make your plans! Adventure is the key here. Know and Go.

September 23 – Fall Equinox – The Sun Moves into Libra

It's harvest time! Count your blessings and know that you have done good work. As the days get shorter, we enter The Time for Embracing, according to the indigenous people, as we experience closer contact with our loved ones and closeness and intimacy become our reality. Snuggle up!

September 27 – Mercury Moves into Scorpio

This brings a challenge in communication. Mercury likes to hang out on the surface of the water when communicating and Scorpio digs deep. Notice if you feel uncomfortable.

September 29 – Venus Enters Libra

Happy days are here again with this combo! Expect a magnetic love attraction to come into play now … enjoy!

Super-Sensitivity – September 2, 3, and 30 ▲

The energy is very fragile, especially around the mind and all of its illusions. Watch what you think, and especially watch what you say. The power of the spoken word is up for recalibration. Beware of misinformation as well as misinterpretation. Think twice, speak once.

Low-Vitality – September 15-16 ▼

Earth changes are very possible right now. Be prepared. Stay close to home, rest, and take special care of your body.

♈ Aries	♋ Cancer	♐ Sagittarius	☽ Moon	♄ Saturn	☊ North Node	V/C Void-of-Course
♉ Taurus	♌ Leo	♑ Capricorn	☿ Mercury	♅ Uranus	☋ South Node	▲ Super-Sensitivity
♊ Gemini	♍ Virgo	♒ Aquarius	♀ Venus	♆ Neptune	➡ Enters	▼ Low-Vitality
	♎ Libra	♓ Pisces	♂ Mars	♇ Pluto	℞ Retrograde	
	♏ Scorpio	☉ Sun	♃ Jupiter	⚷ Chiron	S/D Stationary Direct	

September

Sunday	Monday	Tuesday	Wednesday	Thursday	Friday	Saturday
	1 ♅♆⚷♀℞ Labor Day ☽ V/C 8:39AM ☽→♐ 10:16AM ☿→♎ 10:39PM 3. Your creativity creates abundance.	2 ♅♆⚷♀℞ ▲ 4. Be Patient! It will all work out.	3 ♅♆⚷♀℞ ▲ ☽ V/C 11:06AM ☽→♑ 3:14PM 5. Make progress by adaptability.	4 ♅♆⚷♀℞ 6. Eliminate clutter from your home.	5 ♅♆⚷♀℞ ☽ V/C 8:08AM ☽→♒ 4:58PM ♀→♍ 10:08AM 7. An air of mystery can be exciting.	6 ♅♆⚷♀℞ 8. Never regret extravagance.
7 ♅♆⚷♀℞ ☽ V/C 10:18AM ☽→♓ 4:46PM 9. Unity is key to spiritual awareness.	8 ♅♆⚷♀℞ ○16°♓19′ 6:38PM 10. Use an innovative approach.	9 ♅♆⚷♀℞ ☽ V/C 12:09PM ☽→♈ 4:33PM 2. Gentle attention erases indifference.	10 ♅♆⚷♀℞ ☽ V/C 5:57PM 3. Your optimism inspires others.	11 ♅♆⚷♀℞ ☽→♉ 6:16PM 4. Structure supports change.	12 ♅♆⚷♀℞ 5. There is always a different way out.	13 ♅♆⚷♀℞ ☽ V/C 6:30AM ☽→♊ 11:26PM ♂→♐ 2:58PM 6. Your understanding heals.
14 ♅♆⚷♀℞ 7. Words are a reflection of self.	15 ♅♆⚷♀℞ ▼ ☽ V/C 7:04PM 8. Success is activated by awareness.	16 ♅♆⚷♀℞ ▼ ☽→♋ 8:24AM 9. Stay connected with a loving heart.	17 ♅♆⚷♀℞ 10. Vision the future with spirit.	18 ♅♆⚷♀℞ ☽ V/C 11:38AM ☽→♌ 8:09PM 2. See both sides before choosing.	19 ♅♆⚷♀℞ 3. Socializing is key to a happy life.	20 ♅♆⚷♀℞ ☽ V/C 9:33PM 4. Being economical is a sound plan.
21 ♅♆⚷♀℞ ☽→♍ 8:53AM 5. See where you can be more active.	22 ♅♆⚷℞ Fall Equinox ♀D-10°♑59′ 5:35PM ☉→♎ 7:30PM 6. Sincerity is love in service.	23 ♅♆⚷℞ ●1°♎8′ 11:13PM ☽ V/C 5:14AM ☽→♎ 8:59PM 7. Crossword puzzle, anyone?	24 ♅♆⚷℞ Rosh Hashanah 8. Courage is a gift for success.	25 ♅♆⚷℞ 9. Strive to be consciously aware.	26 ♅♆⚷℞ ☽ V/C 5:38AM ☽→♏ 7:29AM 10. Explore the power of prayer.	27 ♅♆⚷℞ ☿→♏ 3:40PM 2. Polarity is the heart of creation.
28 ♅♆⚷℞ ☽ V/C 1:30PM ☽→♐ 3:50PM 3. Let go. Let life flow through you.	29 ♅♆⚷℞ ▲ ☽ V/C 8:28PM ☽→♒ 6:51AM ♀→♎ 1:53PM 4. Recreate a new working structure.	30 ♅♆⚷℞ ▲ ☽→♑ 9:40PM 5. Master your body through movement.				

Full Moon in Pisces

September 8, 6:38 PM

Degree Choice Points
  16° Pisces 18'

Motivation Inner guidance

Resistance Gullible

Statement I Trust
  Body Feet
  Mind Super-sensitive
  Spirit Mystical

Element
  Water – Feeling, rhythm, living by cycles, flowing, escaping from reality.

First House Moon
  8° Pisces 14'

Motivation Rise and shine

Resistance Boasting

First House Umbrella Theme
  I Am – Your outer appearance, the way you present yourself, the way you dress, the way you enter a room, and what you leave behind when you leave the room.

The Sun is Opposite the Moon

Full Moons are always in opposition to the Sun. This creates a feeling of tension between where you want to shine and how your feelings are flowing on a sensory level about the Sun's directive. The two forces seem like they are working against each other, yet they are on the same team displaying different techniques to attain the same mission. The Pisces/Virgo polarity creates tension between addiction and perfection.

Pisces Goddess

The Pisces goddess, Kuan Yin, is the embodiment of all that is compassionate. She guides us to the abyss, a place known as the "Great Unknown." It is here that the ego drops away and there is only the truth of one's nature. Kuan Yin protects us and holds us when we let go, surrender, and evolve. She is the goddess of emptiness and helps us to constantly empty the self from the limitations of the ego: fear, doubt, guilt, shame, and denial. In exchange, we gain beauty, light, and service. She is often pictured riding on the head of a dragon. It is the breath of the dragon that pierces the veil of illusion.

On Your Altar

Colors Greens, blues, amethyst, aquamarine

Numerology 10 – keep your eye on your goals

Tarot Card The Hanged Man – learning to let go

Gemstones Opal, turquoise, amethyst

Plant remedy Passion flower – the ability to live in the here and now

Fragrance White lotus – connecting to the Divine without arrogance

Meditation

The freedom themes are provided by the zodiac sign and can be from this lifetime or other lifetimes. These meditations assist in dissolving blocks and opening pathways to new frontiers.

When the Moon is in Pisces, take time out to sit quietly. Close your eyes and breathe in and out. Ask the Angel of Records to go with you to see the chaotic regions in the matrix of your mind. See your hidden desires. Look with the eye of compassion to understand where these desires have hurt you or others. Expect a major healing by asking for grace to be given to you while visiting these sordid versions of your past. Make amends with yourself for romanticizing your past and release any escape fantasies that keep you from being present with yourself and with life. Allow yourself to be ignited with your power to heal. Visit hospitals and prisons; offer healings. Focus on your creative, spiritual self.

Pisces Challenges and Victories

Say all of the statements in this section out loud. Then, underline the phrase that means the most to you. Use the phrase as your special affirmation for manifesting and co-creating throughout this phase of the moon.

The best thing I can do for myself today is to get out of the way, so life can take its own course without the interference of my control drama. I take time out to let go and let things be. I have become too involved in the details and have lost sight of the vastness of the Universe, and the infinite possibilities that are available to me at all times and in every moment. I am aware that all I need is a different way of seeing what I have perceived as a problem, and that my view is limited by my needs, rather than by accepting things as they are. I trust that, when I get out of the way and give space to the power of NOW, all is in Divine Order and everything works out for the good of all concerned. This is the day when doing nothing gets me everything. I allow myself to experience the void. I empty myself of my rigidity, small-mindedness, racing thoughts, the need to be right, and to control outcomes. I know that non-action will present me with right action. I give the Universe a chance and trust the view to be larger than mine. When I accept myself as I am, I learn what I can become. I remove myself from all of the mind chatter and allow for silence to do its work. I am aware that a quiet mind brings me peace (the absence of conflict). In turning upside down, I see how right-side-up things really are. Acceptance brings me perspective. Acceptance sets me free. Acceptance brings me wholeness. Acceptance widens my mind.

Pisces Homework

Get a foot massage to bring your energy back to the ground. Feel the power of your path on the bottom of your feet. Now that you are back to your body, it is time to make a list of the ways your boundaries get breached. After the completion of your list, read it out loud and then throw it in the ocean. Now it is time to see the seed of life, the seed of love, and the seed of power that were planted into the womb of evolution.

Full Moon in Pisces

September 8, 6:38 PM

Clearing the Slate for Freedom

Remember a time when you experienced the following trigger points. Write down what happened, forgive yourself, release it, and let it go to clear your slate for freedom.

Unrealistic

- Forgive
- Release
- Let go

Escape Dramas

- Forgive
- Release
- Let go

Addictions

- Forgive
- Release
- Let go

Emotionally Unreliable

- Forgive
- Release
- Let go

Aimless

- Forgive
- Release
- Let go

My Freedom List

Pisces Freedom List Ideas

Now is the time to set myself free from addictions, illusions and fantasy, escape dramas, martyrdom, victimhood, and mental chaos.

Full Moon in Pisces

September 8, 6:38 PM

How to Use the Moon Book With Your Chart

Fill in the blanks on the Cosmic Check-In page. Then look up the degree of the moon on the chart below. Take note of the "I" statement on the outside of the wheel where the moon is located. Now locate the same degree on your own chart, and make a note of the house and corresponding "I" statement. Go back to the Cosmic Check-In page and circle the two statements from the charts and read what you wrote. This will give you an idea about what to expect from this moon phase on a personal level.

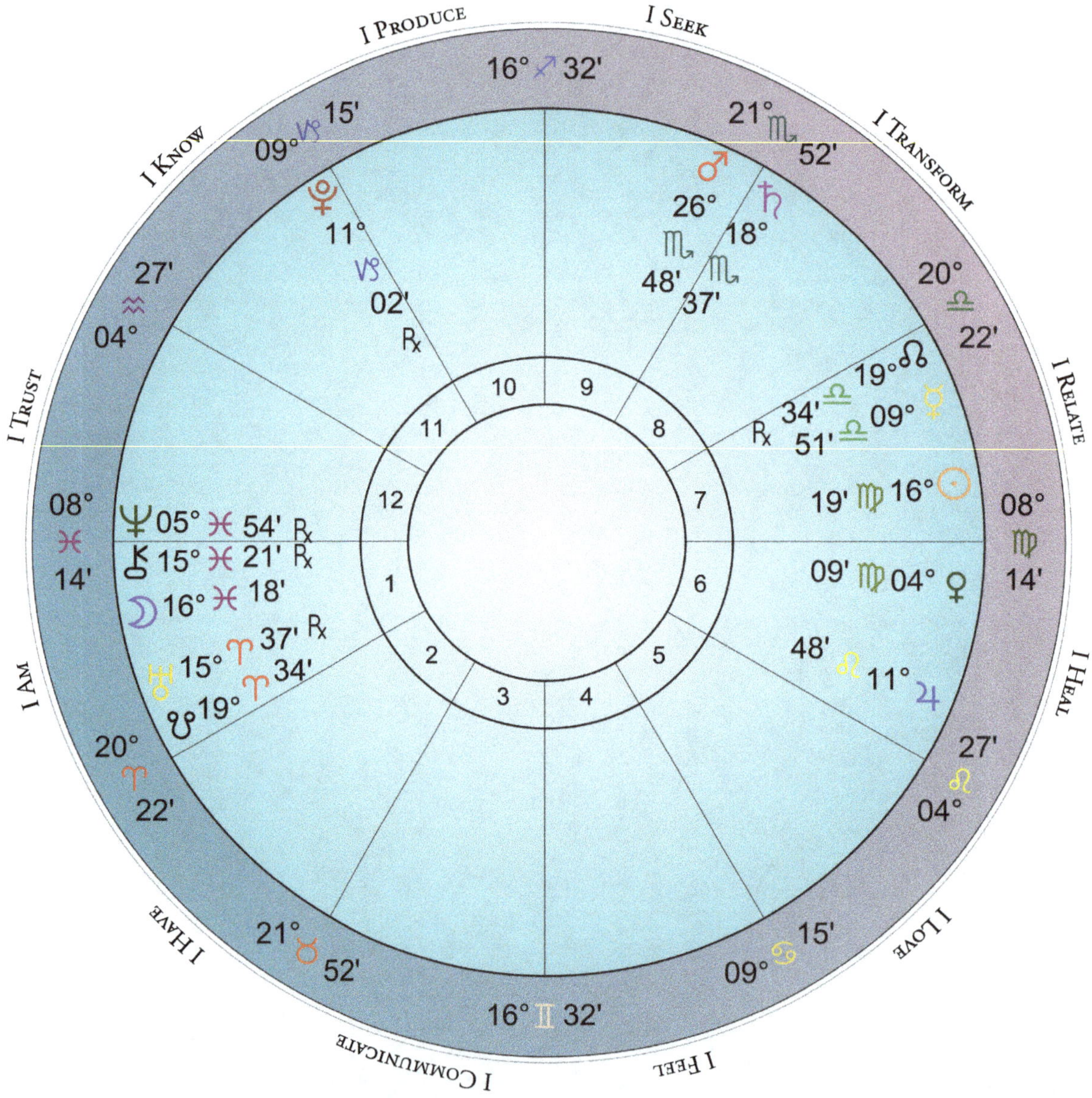

♈ Aries	♋ Cancer	♐ Sagittarius	☽ Moon	♄ Saturn	☊ North Node	V/C Void-of-Course
♉ Taurus	♌ Leo	♑ Capricorn	☿ Mercury	♅ Uranus	☋ South Node	▲ Super-Sensitivity
♊ Gemini	♍ Virgo	♒ Aquarius	♀ Venus	♆ Neptune	➡ Enters	▼ Low-Vitality
	♎ Libra	♓ Pisces	♂ Mars	♇ Pluto	℞ Retrograde	
	♏ Scorpio	☉ Sun	♃ Jupiter	⚷ Chiron	S/D Stationary Direct	

Cosmic Check-In

Take a moment to write a brief phrase for each "I" statement.
This activates all areas of your life for this creative cycle.

♓ I Trust

♈ I Am

♉ I Have

♊ I Communicate

♋ I Feel

♌ I Love

♍ I Heal

♎ I Relate

♏ I Transform

♐ I Seek

♑ I Produce

♒ I Know

New Moon in Libra

September 23, 11:13 PM

Degree Choice Points
 1° Libra 08'

Motivation Evolving social vision

Resistance Impracticality

Statement I Relate
 Body Kidneys
 Mind Social
 Spirit Peace

Element
 Air – Bridges the mundane to the divine, promotes curiosity, insights, and perspectives.

Fourth House Moon
 7° Virgo 24'

Motivation Multi-tasking

Resistance Awkwardness

Fourth House Umbrella Theme
 I Feel – The way your early environmental training was, how that set your foundation for living, and why you chose your mother.

When the Sun is in Libra

Libra energy gives us the opportunity to bridge the gap between the higher and lower mind; abstract thinking versus concrete thinking. During Libra time, the light and dark forces are in balance and we are given a chance to experience harmony. Harmony occurs when we keep our polarities in motion and put paradox to rest, thus breaking the crystallization of polarity. Now is the time to weigh our values through the light of our soul. Libra asks us to look at what is increasing and decreasing in our lives. Start with friendship, courage, sincerity, and understanding, and keep going until your scale is in motion.

Libra Goddess

The whole idea of Libra is to weigh and measure decreasing and increasing light. The goddess best known for the ability to measure light is Ma'at. Ma'at has the ability to weigh and measure frequencies of a light heart or a heavy one. According to Egyptian mythology, it is Ma'at who waits at the gateway to the other side and measures the lightness of being in order to determine the direction one is to take when entering the Underworld. Ma'at's symbol for measurement is an ostrich plume. Each heart that enters must be weighed and be in balance against her feather. If the heart is heavy, it is determined by Ma'at that the soul must transition to an area known as the darker world. If the heart is light and balanced with her feather, the soul is directed to the lighter world. Because of this process, she began to make her contribution to civilization by holding the space for cosmic balance, right order, and natural law.

On Your Altar

Colors Pink, green

Numerology 8 – we prosper by sharing

Tarot Card Justice – the Law of Cause and Effect

Gemstones Jade, rose quartz

Plant Remedy Olive trees – stamina

Fragrance Eucalyptus – clarity of breath

My Co-Creation List

Libra Co-Creation Ideas

Now is the time to focus on manifesting relationships, wholeness, being loving, lovable, and loved, living life as an art form, balance and equality, integrity, accuracy, diplomacy, and peace.

This, or something better than this, comes to me in an easy and pleasurable way for the good of all concerned. Thank you, Universe!

New Moon in Libra

September 23, 11:13 PM

Libra Challenges and Victories

Say all of the statements in this section out loud. Then, underline the phrase that means the most to you. Use the phrase as your special affirmation for manifesting and co-creating throughout this phase of the moon.

I feel the call of the higher worlds awakening me to a new vibration. This call is to move beyond judgment and move to a place of acceptance, understanding, unconditional confidence, and love. I am at a place in my life where I can embrace the world of acceptance and wholeness, because I have birthed myself anew, beyond the imprisonment and crystallization of polarity and righteousness. My black and white worlds of right and wrong have integrated and blended into gray, the color of wisdom, where true knowledge exists. Knowledge simply is, and the need for proof does not exist where wisdom lives.

The only requirement is experience. I know that everything that comes before me is a direct reflection of my own experience and, in embracing this concept, I can now receive the gift of infinite awareness. I am in a place of awareness that came before and goes beyond where good and evil exist. I have within me, the presence of unconditional confidence to go where true love lives. I no longer need to prove myself. I am now simply being myself. I release the need to be right and accept the right to BE. I no longer need to be forgiven, because I am neither wrong nor right. I no longer need to define myself. Acceptance has no reason for defense. I no longer need to be guilty; duty motivation is no longer a reality. I know that where there is judgment, there is separation. I know understanding unifies. I accept the call of the higher worlds and express myself freely and fully without fear of judgment. I accept myself as I am, so I can learn what I can become.

Libra Homework

Libra co-creates best through the legal industry, beauty industry, diplomatic service, match-making, urban development, mediation, feng shui, spa ownership, clutter busting and space clearing, romance writing, wedding consulting, fashion design, and as a librarian.

It is time to weigh and measure the values of relationship, friendship, courage, sensitivity, sincerity, and understanding. Look at what is increasing and what is decreasing in these areas.

Without Acknowledgment Progress Cannot Occur

Acknowledgment creates space for victory and gratitude, which automatically brings us to a level of completion so a new cycle of opportunity can occur in our lives. When we celebrate our wins and acknowledge our victories with gratitude, we update our cells so that our ability to move forward is not hindered by a cellular holographic pattern that is stuck in the past. Cellular lag creates resistance and makes moving forward most difficult. The key is to stay continuously updated by acknowledging yourself for what you did do at the end of each day rather than heading off to sleep thinking about what you did not do. By acknowledging what we didn't do, we play into our karmic storage bank and keep our progress at bay. When we acknowledge ourselves and our manifestations, we are complete, and more cycles of opportunity become available to us in each new day. Be prepared for miracles.

Victory List

Gratitude List

This fulfills the relationship between the giver and the receiver, which completes the cycle with the Universe so that a new beginning can be established.

New Moon in Libra

September 23, 11:13 PM

How to Use the Moon Book With Your Chart

Fill in the blanks on the Cosmic Check-In page. Then look up the degree of the moon on the chart below. Take note of the "I" statement on the outside of the wheel where the moon is located. Now locate the same degree on your own chart, and make a note of the house and corresponding "I" statement. Go back to the Cosmic Check-In page and circle the two statements from the charts and read what you wrote. This will give you an idea about what to expect from this moon phase on a personal level.

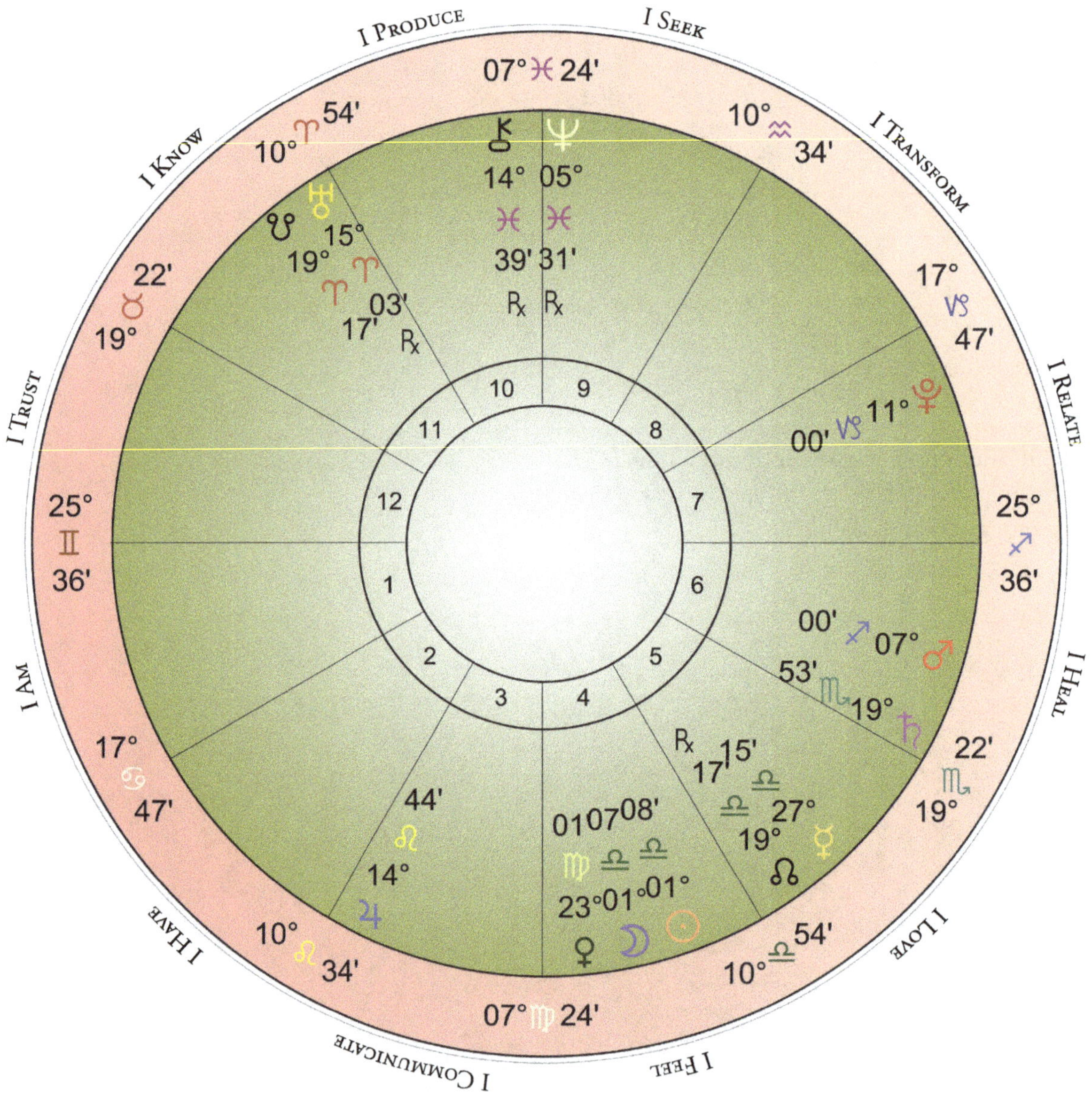

♈ Aries	♋ Cancer	♐ Sagittarius	☽ Moon	♄ Saturn	☊ North Node	V/C Void-of-Course
♉ Taurus	♌ Leo	♑ Capricorn	☿ Mercury	♅ Uranus	☋ South Node	▲ Super-Sensitivity
♊ Gemini	♍ Virgo	♒ Aquarius	♀ Venus	♆ Neptune	➡ Enters	▼ Low-Vitality
	♎ Libra	♓ Pisces	♂ Mars	♇ Pluto	℞ Retrograde	
	♏ Scorpio	☉ Sun	♃ Jupiter	⚷ Chiron	S/D Stationary Direct	

Cosmic Check-In

Take a moment to write a brief phrase for each "I" statement. This activates all areas of your life for this creative cycle.

♎ I Relate

♏ I Transform

♐ I Seek

♑ I Produce

♒ I Know

♓ I Trust

♈ I Am

♉ I Have

♊ I Communicate

♋ I Feel

♌ I Love

♍ I Heal

October Planetary Highlights

Uranus Continues to be Retrograde in Aries for the Entire Month

Expect impulsiveness and rebellion in order to update limiting social values and approaches to education and communication. Do a check-up on your intellectual snobbery or elitism and see where you may need to widen your periphery.

Neptune Continues to be Retrograde in Pisces for the Entire Month

We can expect to approach our lives from the space of high ideals. This is a time to do a check on your moral principles, ideals, and personal truth, in order to move beyond collective affirmations that inhibit the individual's progress by promoting fear, limitation, and disrespect.

Chiron Continues to be Retrograde in Pisces for the Entire Month

Take some time this month to recognize where your wounds are. When we identify our wounds, Chiron can come forward with the appropriate way to heal them. Start by asking yourself, "Where am I angry with God?" Now is the time to heal your relationship with the Divine and to become free to make choices beyond survival.

Mercury goes Retrograde in Scorpio – October 4

Mercury is the messenger and feels trapped while visiting Scorpio. Pay attention to this entrapped feeling in yourself and open up to receive a message to work on during this time.

Uranus in Aries and the Sun in Libra Face Off in Exact Opposition – October 7

This brings on a restless duel between the idea of new potential coming forward, without rebellion, and the part of you that wants to keep things the same. If you go for the new potential, it will become a long range reality worth celebrating.

Lunar Eclipse – Pluto/Uranus Standoff – Mars and Jupiter Trine – October 8

Expect a major positive influence to be felt on national and global levels as this cycle comes to completion.

Mercury Makes a Replay and Backs into Libra – October 10

This is a time to mind your manners, no matter how rough it gets.

The Sun Moves into Scorpio – October 23

It's time to shine your light on the darker versions of your personality and transform them.

Venus Moves into Scorpio – Oct. 23

Expect jealousy and possessiveness to enter your consciousness. Do what you can to not act on these emotions. Right now, there are five planets in water signs and it's a good idea to contain your feelings.

Mercury goes Direct in Libra – October 25

Expect indecisiveness to come up and many changes to occur in your plans.

Low-Vitality – October 12-13 ▼

Things are ending all around you during these days. Do your best to let them end, and don't waste your energy holding onto what no longer has any life force. Your vitality is more important than anything. Do what it takes to be balanced.

Super-Sensitivity – October 20, 24, 27-28 ▲

Pay attention to outside influences. The atmosphere is filled with negative thoughts, depression, and fear. Do your best to stay centered in your own process, so you don't buy into the toxic, global energy field.

♈ Aries	♋ Cancer	♐ Sagittarius	☽ Moon	♄ Saturn	☊ North Node	V/C Void-of-Course
♉ Taurus	♌ Leo	♑ Capricorn	☿ Mercury	♅ Uranus	☋ South Node	▲ Super-Sensitivity
♊ Gemini	♍ Virgo	♒ Aquarius	♀ Venus	♆ Neptune	➡ Enters	▼ Low-Vitality
	♎ Libra	♓ Pisces	♂ Mars	♇ Pluto	℞ Retrograde	
	♏ Scorpio	☉ Sun	♃ Jupiter	⚷ Chiron	S/D Stationary Direct	

October

Sunday	Monday	Tuesday	Wednesday	Thursday	Friday	Saturday
			1 ♅♆⚷℞ 6. Maintain a harmonious home.	**2** ♅♆⚷℞ ☽ V/C 9:17AM 7. Look within to find your truth.	**3** ♅♆⚷℞ Yom Kippur ☽→♒ 12:59AM 8. Choose to be successful.	**4** ☿♅♆⚷℞ ☽ V/C 11:32AM ☿℞-2°♏18' 10:03AM 9. Interact with a spirit of love.
5 ☿♅♆⚷℞ ☽→♓ 2:24AM 10. Endings create new beginnings.	**6** ☿♅♆⚷℞ ☽ V/C 12:38AM 2. Make a decision that brings peace.	**7** ☿♅♆⚷℞ ☽→♈ 3:06AM 3. Living in the past is not creative.	**8** ☿♅♆⚷℞ ○15°♈5' 3:50AM Lunar Eclipse 3:54AM ☽ V/C 7:20AM 4. Intuition gets the best results.	**9** ☿♅♆⚷℞ ☽→♉ 4:43AM 5. All fear restricts your energy.	**10** ☿♅♆⚷℞ ☽ V/C 5:48PM ☿℞→♎-10:28AM 6. An open hearted attitude works best.	**11** ☿♅♆⚷℞ ☽→♊ 8:50AM 7. Fear is a result of negative thinking.
12 ☿♅♆⚷℞ ▼ 8. See unlimited possibilities.	**13** ☿♅♆⚷℞ ▼ Columbus Day ☽ V/C 10:58AM ☽→♋ 4:30PM 9. Thinking green entails green action.	**14** ☿♅♆⚷℞ 10. To begin requires new attitude.	**15** ☿♅♆⚷℞ ☽ V/C 4:26PM 2. Decide and don't look back.	**16** ☿♅♆⚷℞ ☽→♌ 3:29AM 3. Find joy in artistic expression.	**17** ☿♅♆⚷℞ 4. Without a base, nothing lasts.	**18** ☿♅♆⚷℞ ☽ V/C 6:09AM ☽→♍ 4:07PM 5. Embrace change as your friend.
19 ☿♅♆⚷℞ ▲ 6. Peace and harmony make a home.	**20** ☿♅♆⚷℞ ▲ ☽ V/C 8:29PM 8. Be discriminating in your choices.	**21** ☿♅♆⚷℞ ▲ ☽→♎ 4:11AM 9. Pray for someone's good.	**22** ☿♅♆⚷℞ ▲ 10. Choose happiness now.	**23** ☿♅♆⚷℞ ▲ ●0°♏25' 2:56 PM Solar Eclipse 2:43PM ☽ V/C 10:21AM ☽→♏ 2:09PM ☉→♏ 4:58AM ♀→♏ 1:53PM 2. Think both/and instead of either/or.	**24** ☿♅♆⚷℞ ▲ 3. Adapt a playful attitude.	**25** ♅♆⚷℞ ☽ V/C 9:11AM ☽→♐ 9:39PM ☿D-16°♎46'-12:18PM 4. Detach from the outcome.
26 ♅♆⚷℞ ♂→♑ 3:44AM 5. Expand perceptions to change.	**27** ♅♆⚷℞ ▲ ☽ V/C 9:18AM 6. Create a special sacred place.	**28** ♅♆⚷℞ ▲ ☽→♑ 3:03AM 7. It's ok to think outside the box.	**29** ♅♆⚷℞ ☽ V/C 8:00PM 8. Your only limits are self created.	**30** ♅♆⚷℞ ☽→♒ 6:51AM 9. Your prayers make a difference.	**31** ♅♆⚷℞ Halloween ☽ V/C 11:21PM 10. Replace the old with the new.	

Full Moon in Aries

October 8, 3:50 AM – Full Moon in Aries – Lunar Eclipse

The Sun is Opposite the Moon

Full Moons are always in opposition to the Sun. This creates a feeling of tension between where you want to shine and how your feelings are flowing on a sensory level about the Sun's directive. The two forces seem like they are working against each other, yet they are on the same team displaying different techniques to attain the same goal. The Aries/Libra polarity creates tension between "I Am" and "We Are."

Aries God

Mars is the god of war. His statement is, "I fight." Before going into battle, Mars required something to be sacrificed on the eve of the battle. When he went into battle, he traveled with two gods: Deimos, god of terror, and Phobos, god of fear. They symbolized the unconscious elements of war. It never mattered to Mars on which side of the war he fought; it was the battle itself that seduced him. When the Moon is full in Aries, we are given the opportunity to examine the inner conflict. Where are we at war with our Self, our relationships, and our environment? Questions to ask yourself: Is my anger worth the sacrifice? What am I sacrificing in order to stay angry?

On Your Altar

Colors Red, black, coral

Numerology 4 – organize yourself

Tarot Card Tower – release from a stuck place, a major breakthrough

Gemstones Diamond, red jasper, coral, obsidian

Plant remedy Oak, pomegranate – planting new life and rooting new life

Fragrance Ginger – the ability to ingest and digest life

Degree Choice Points
   15° Aries 04'

Motivation Help from the invisible

Resistance Self-deception

Statement I Am
   Body Head
   Mind Impulsive
   Spirit Initiation

Element
   Fire – Inspiration, action, initiation, passion, enthusiasm, the Divine Masculine, "my way or the highway."

Eighth House Moon
   2° Aries 09'

Motivation Acceptance

Resistance Stereotyping

Eighth House Umbrella Theme
   I Transform – How you share money and other resources, what you keep hidden regarding sex, death, real estate, and regeneration.

Meditation

The freedom themes are provided by the zodiac sign and can be from this lifetime or other lifetimes. These meditations assist in dissolving blocks and opening pathways to new frontiers.

When the Moon is in Aries, it is a time to face irritability issues relating to challenge, hostility, impatience, and war. Sit quietly and close your eyes, breathe in and breathe out and look in the memory banks for times when you forced your will on others, and reconcile with the old warrior that you were. Open the pathway to becoming the peaceful warrior who expresses without impatience or the impulse of battle. Take action, be energized, and focus on yourself. Know that you have the power to work things out with clear self-expression. Continue to see yourself clearly, without the interfering definitions of others.

Aries Challenges and Victories

Say all of the statements in this section out loud. Then, underline the phrase that means the most to you. Use the phrase as your special affirmation for manifesting and co-creating throughout this phase of the moon.

Today, I let go. I trust that whatever breaks down or breaks through is a blessing in disguise for me. I make a commitment to allow myself to be spontaneous and live in the moment. I know the unexpected is a blessing for me and a way for me to make a breakthrough out of my limitations. I am aware that I am resistant to change. I know I must make changes and am too stubborn to take the appropriate action myself to change. I have built many walls of false protection around me, guarding me and blocking me from the reality that change is a constant. I have freeze-framed my life and desire support to update myself. I have allowed my fear of change to become my false motto and my life is at a standstill. I am unwilling use any more energy to perpetuate my resistance. I know that continuing to cling to the past is a waste of my energy. I can no longer put things off that delay my process. I feel the breaking down of form. I trust that all changes are in my favor. All changes lead me to golden opportunities. I release false pride. I release false foundations. I release false authorities. In so doing, I allow for everything to crumble around me so I can see that my true strength is within and I will build my life from the inside out.

I am ready for new experiences. I am ready for the unexpected. I am willing to have an event occur so I can become activated towards my breakthrough. I am ready for the power of now. I know being spontaneous will bring me to true joy. I know if I ride this carrier wave it will take me to a place far beyond my scope of limited thinking. I know the will of God works in my favor and knows more than I do in any given moment.

Aries Homework

Now you are ready to take a personal inventory on behaviors such as impatience, talking over people, brat attacks, and starting every sentence with "I."

This is a time when the light becomes a prisoner of polarized forces. This diminishing light begins its yearly sojourn beneath the surface asking us to balance light and dark by mastering the concept of equilibrium. Equilibrium is the Law of Harmony, where we attempt to reach a state of achievement by combining paradoxical fields that break the crystallization of polarity. Spend time looking for increasing and decreasing fields of light around you.

Full Moon in Aries

October 8, 3:50 AM – Full Moon in Aries – Lunar Eclipse

Clearing the Slate for Freedom

Remember a time when you experienced the following trigger points. Write down what happened, forgive yourself, release it, and let it go to clear your slate for freedom.

Anger

- Forgive
- Release
- Let go

The Need to Be First

- Forgive
- Release
- Let go

Arrogance

- Forgive
- Release
- Let go

Impatience

- Forgive
- Release
- Let go

Forceful

- Forgive
- Release
- Let go

My Freedom List

Aries Freedom List Ideas

Now is the time to set myself free from anger that is toxic, competition and comparison, irritation and struggle, the need to be first, overdoing it and not resting, impatience, impulsiveness, challenge, and hostility.

Full Moon in Aries

October 8, 3:50 AM – Full Moon in Aries – Lunar Eclipse

How to Use the Moon Book With Your Chart

Fill in the blanks on the Cosmic Check-In page. Then look up the degree of the moon on the chart below. Take note of the "I" statement on the outside of the wheel where the moon is located. Now locate the same degree on your own chart, and make a note of the house and corresponding "I" statement. Go back to the Cosmic Check-In page and circle the two statements from the charts and read what you wrote. This will give you an idea about what to expect from this moon phase on a personal level.

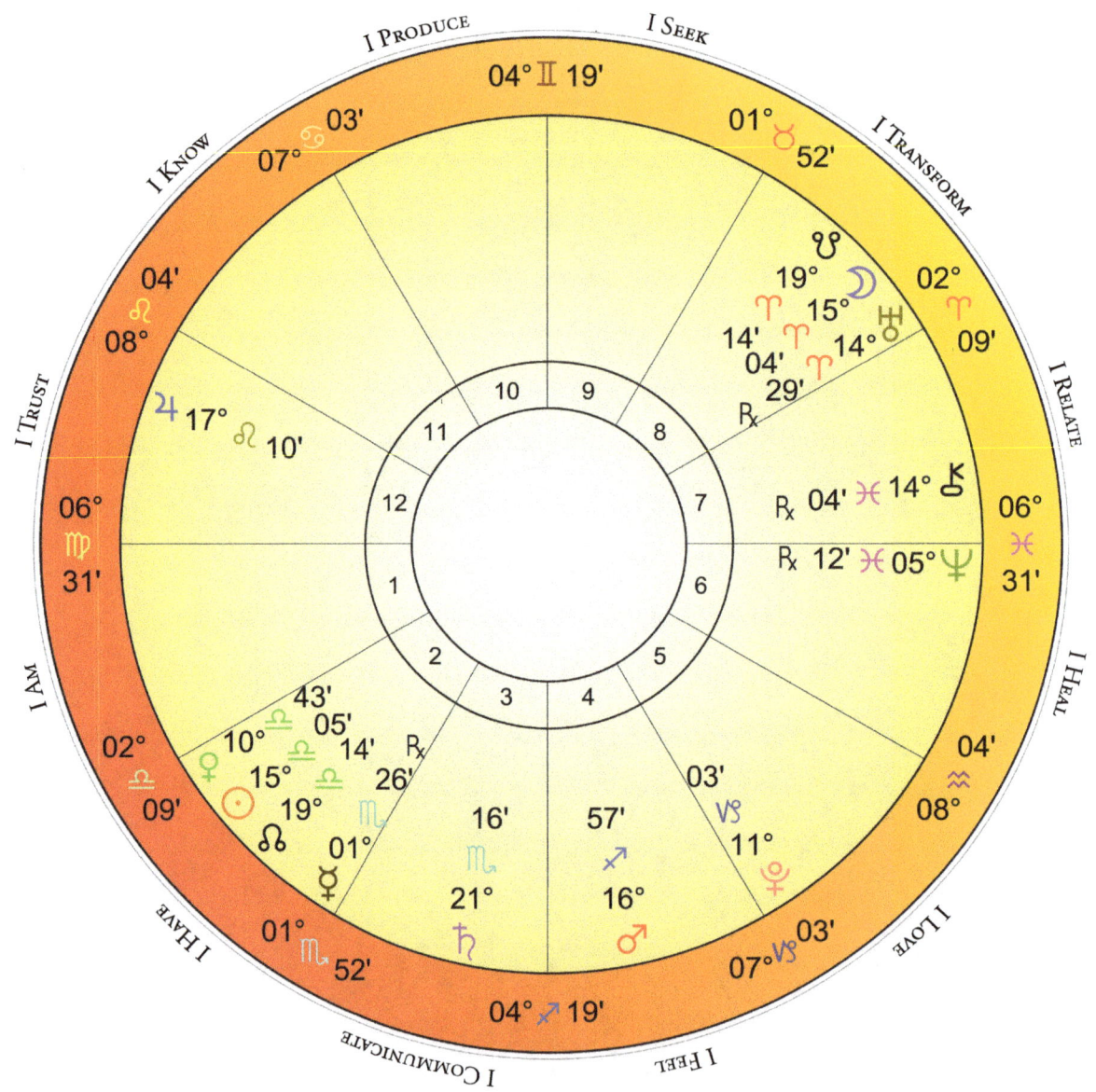

♈ Aries	♋ Cancer	♐ Sagittarius	☽ Moon	♄ Saturn	☊ North Node	V/C Void-of-Course
♉ Taurus	♌ Leo	♑ Capricorn	☿ Mercury	♅ Uranus	☋ South Node	▲ Super-Sensitivity
♊ Gemini	♍ Virgo	♒ Aquarius	♀ Venus	♆ Neptune	➡ Enters	▼ Low-Vitality
	♎ Libra	♓ Pisces	♂ Mars	♇ Pluto	℞ Retrograde	
	♏ Scorpio	☉ Sun	♃ Jupiter	⚷ Chiron	S/D Stationary Direct	

Cosmic Check-In

Take a moment to write a brief phrase for each "I" statement. This activates all areas of your life for this creative cycle.

♈ I Am

♉ I Have

♊ I Communicate

♋ I Feel

♌ I Love

♍ I Heal

♎ I Relate

♏ I Transform

♐ I Seek

♑ I Produce

♒ I Know

♓ I Trust

New Moon in Scorpio

October 23, 2:56 PM – Solar Eclipse

When the Sun is in Scorpio

Scorpio is the symbol of darkness which heralds the decline of the Sun in Autumn. Scorpio embodies the Law of Nature, which decrees that even the strongest will must bow to the body's mortality. As we watch all of nature going through a slow death, we begin to recognize the qualities of Scorpio's subtlety and depth, and the hidden forces that threaten those who live only on the surface. Scorpio rules all of the things that we try to keep hidden: death, taxes, power, money, sex, resentment, revenge, ambition, pride, and fear. When we face these self-imposed limits in ourselves, we take on the true power of transformation. Transformation establishes pathways for us to decentralize the ego in the interest of higher humanitarian work.

Scorpio Goddess

Persephone, the goddess of the Underworld, is assigned to Scorpio. During the time of Scorpio, all of nature begins its sojourn into darkness in preparation for the void that comes in winter. Persephone is the harbinger of the Sun's decline. It is Persephone who asks us to release the idea of living on the surface in order to quest for the depth of our hidden forces, to recharge, rejuvenate, transform, and let go. Persephone rules our intuition, our inner beauty, the occult arts, and our ability to accept the cycles in nature that support our fertility, even when the cycle feels like death. Her domain comes alive in us every time we close our eyes. When the Moon is new in Scorpio, ask Persephone to guide you below the surface.

On Your Altar

Colors Deep red, black, deep purple

Numerology 2 – balance and harmony are the way to go

Tarot Card Death – the ability to transform, transmute, and transcend

Gemstones Topaz, smoky quartz, obsidian, jet, onyx

Plant Remedy Manzanita – being open to transforming cycles

Fragrance Sandalwood – awakens your sensuality

Degree Choice Points
0° Scorpio 25'

Motivation Attentive

Resistance Outsider

Statement I Transform
Body Sex organs
Mind Intensity
Spirit Transformation

Element
Water – Intense, passionate, sexual, powerful, focused, controlling, deep, driven, secretive.

Eighth House Moon
5° Libra 27'

Motivation Manifesting a vision

Resistance Invoking negatives

Eighth House Umbrella Theme
I Transform – How you share money and other resources, what you keep hidden regarding sex, death, real estate, and regeneration.

My Co-Creation List

Scorpio Co-Creation Ideas

Now is the time to focus on manifesting transformation on all levels, bringing light to the dark, knowing and living cycles, knowing trust as an option, accepting change, accepting my sexuality, knowing sex is natural, knowing sex as good, and knowing sex as creative.

This, or something better than this, comes to me in an easy and pleasurable way for the good of all concerned. Thank you, Universe!

New Moon in Scorpio

October 23, 2:56 PM – Solar Eclipse

Scorpio Challenges and Victories

Say all of the statements in this section out loud. Then, underline the phrase that means the most to you. Use the phrase as your special affirmation for manifesting and co-creating throughout this phase of the moon.

"When the student needs to learn, the teacher appears." Today, I recognize that the Law of Reflection is in operation. I have become aware of this through my over-indulgence of judgment and criticism of other people. I am aware that when my judgment is running rampant, I am in need of a teacher who can interpret this judgment as reflection, so I can see my judgments as my teachers and use them to re-interpret myself. I seek counsel with someone who has the ability to listen to me, hear me, and give me the space I need to see myself. I have become confused by spending too much time looking outside of myself for the answers. Perhaps my authority systems, like my religion or my family traditions, no longer serve me and I need to use this confusion to become aware of a new, more self-reliant way to live my life.

The Law of Reflection

Whatever I judge is what I am, what I fear, or what I lack. I make a list of my judgments:

I rewrite each judgment in the form of a question: Am I _____? Do I fear _____? Do I lack _____?

Example 1: I judge Mary's wealth. Do I fear wealth? Do I lack wealth? Am I wealthy in my own way and forgetting to acknowledge my own ability to manifest?

Example 2: I judge John's "be perfect" attitude. Do I fear perfection? Do I lack perfection? Have I forgotten to recognize my own perfection?

In moving through this process, I reconnect to myself and find my own authority today. I send blessings to others whose reflection has so beautifully shown me myself today. I now know and cherish my judgments as my greatest teachers and set myself free today.

Scorpio Homework

Scorpio co-creates best by being a private investigator, detective, probate attorney, mystery writer, mythologist, tarot reader, symbolist, hospice worker, transition counselor, mortician, sex surrogate, or in forensic medicine.

The Scorpio Moon cycle asks us to transform. In order to do this we must transmute sex drive into creativity, physical comfort into serving the greater good, money into higher value, fear into light, animosity into understanding, ambition into service to beauty, pride into humility, separation into unity, control into harmony, and power into empowerment.

Without Acknowledgment Progress Cannot Occur

Acknowledgment creates space for victory and gratitude, which automatically brings us to a level of completion so a new cycle of opportunity can occur in our lives. When we celebrate our wins and acknowledge our victories with gratitude, we update our cells so that our ability to move forward is not hindered by a cellular holographic pattern that is stuck in the past. Cellular lag creates resistance and makes moving forward most difficult. The key is to stay continuously updated by acknowledging yourself for what you did do at the end of each day rather than heading off to sleep thinking about what you did not do. By acknowledging what we didn't do, we play into our karmic storage bank and keep our progress at bay. When we acknowledge ourselves and our manifestations, we are complete, and more cycles of opportunity become available to us in each new day. Be prepared for miracles.

Victory List

Gratitude List

This fulfills the relationship between the giver and the receiver, which completes the cycle with the Universe so that a new beginning can be established.

New Moon in Scorpio

October 23, 2:56 PM – Solar Eclipse

How to Use the Moon Book With Your Chart

Fill in the blanks on the Cosmic Check-In page. Then look up the degree of the moon on the chart below. Take note of the "I" statement on the outside of the wheel where the moon is located. Now locate the same degree on your own chart, and make a note of the house and corresponding "I" statement. Go back to the Cosmic Check-In page and circle the two statements from the charts and read what you wrote. This will give you an idea about what to expect from this moon phase on a personal level.

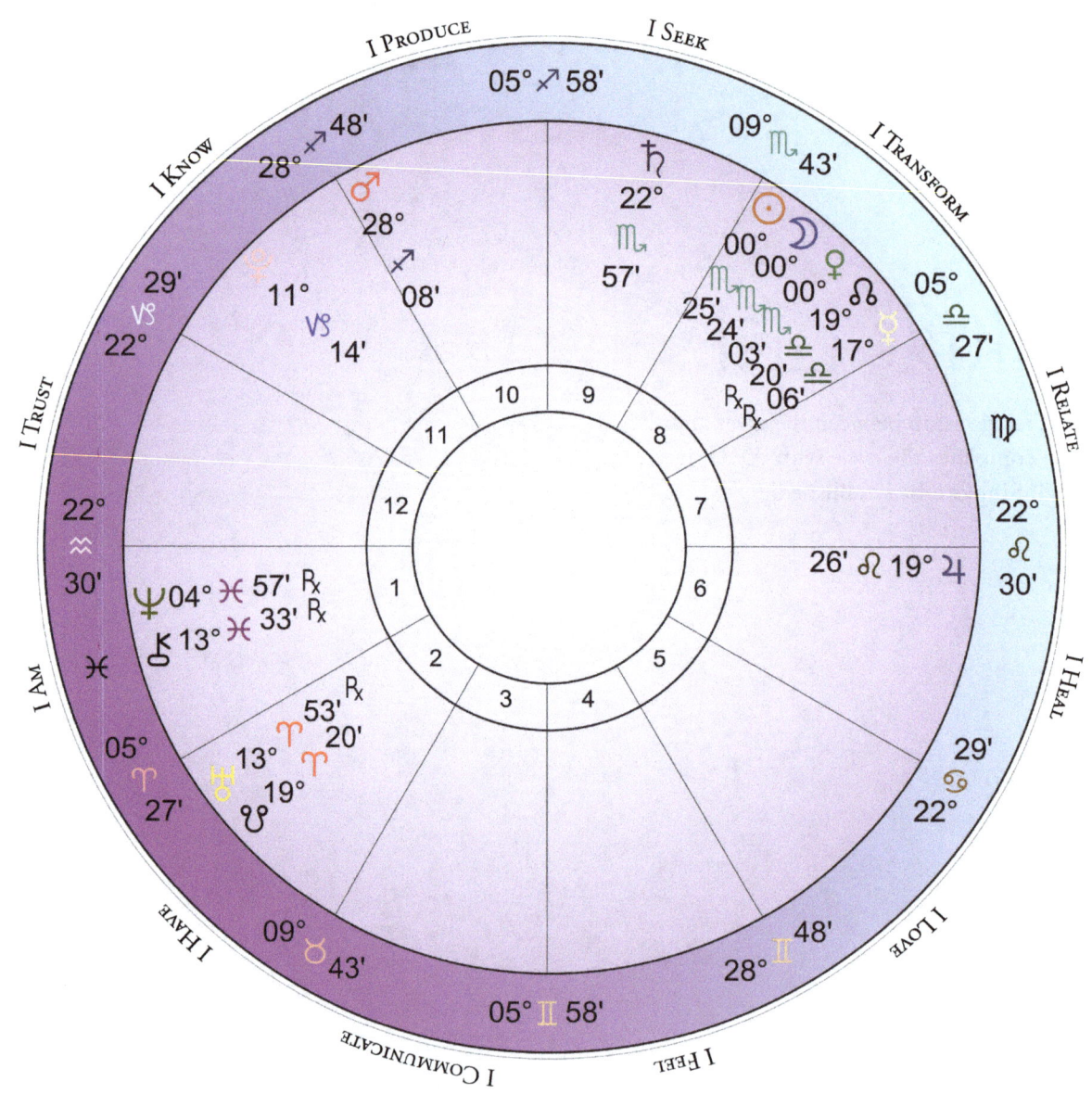

♈ Aries	♋ Cancer	♐ Sagittarius	☽ Moon	♄ Saturn	☊ North Node	V/C Void-of-Course
♉ Taurus	♌ Leo	♑ Capricorn	☿ Mercury	♅ Uranus	☋ South Node	▲ Super-Sensitivity
♊ Gemini	♍ Virgo	♒ Aquarius	♀ Venus	♆ Neptune	➡ Enters	▼ Low-Vitality
	♎ Libra	♓ Pisces	♂ Mars	♇ Pluto	℞ Retrograde	
	♏ Scorpio		☉ Sun	⚷ Chiron	S/D Stationary Direct	

196

Cosmic Check-In

Take a moment to write a brief phrase for each "I" statement.
This activates all areas of your life for this creative cycle.

♏ I Transform

♐ I Seek

♑ I Produce

♒ I Know

♓ I Trust

♈ I Am

♉ I Have

♊ I Communicate

♋ I Feel

♌ I Love

♍ I Heal

♎ I Relate

November Planetary Highlights

Uranus Continues to be Retrograde in Aries for the Entire Month

The key here is to let instability do its work. Be spontaneous and learn to live in the power of the present, rather than clinging to what you think you already know. When the ground is shaky, you are being presented with the gift of something new. Do a reality test on yourself this month to see how willing you are to hold progress in the palm of your hand.

Neptune goes Direct in Pisces – November 15

This is a time to do some serious clearing on yourself to clean the slate of whatever disappointments, disillusions, betrayals, resentments, and denials are in the way of your personal expansion. There is a tendency this month to focus on revenge and addiction, rather than forgiveness. It is now time to release and transmute. If there is a memory that haunts you and you have trouble releasing this memory, write a story about what happened to you in the third person. This will get your ego out of the way to create space for a healing to occur. Then make a list. Start with the sentence: "I release and forgive _____." Last, but definitely not least, remember to forgive yourself! Say it out loud. The goal here is to create space for the new, so expansion can become a reality.

Chiron goes Direct in Pisces – November 23

Ask yourself, "Did I locate my wounds and set up a conscious plan to heal them?" If not, make a plan before the 23rd.

Mercury Enters Scorpio – November 8

Expect communications to be pointed, secretive, under the radar, and manipulative.

Venus Moves into Sagittarius – November 16

This is a time for fun, play, and parties. Expect an adventure to come forward and make you happy!

The Sun Moves into Sagittarius – November 22

Have a blast connecting to your Soul goals and celebrate making life happen!! Adventure is in the air, go traveling. Avoid exaggerating and losing sight of the details.

Mercury Enters Sagittarius – November 27

Expect to talk a lot and to laugh a lot; the louder, the better! Enthusiasm is in the air—enjoy!

Low-Vitality – November 8-9 ▼

Check your resistance levels and see where they are adding tension to the body. Practice the idea of letting go of what doesn't energize you and seek out new avenues for nurturing.

Super-Sensitivity – November 23-24 ▲

Take the time to monitor your stress levels and be aware of outside influences that could sweep you off of your path at this time.

♈ Aries	♋ Cancer	♐ Sagittarius	☽ Moon	♄ Saturn	☊ North Node	V/C Void-of-Course
♉ Taurus	♌ Leo	♑ Capricorn	☿ Mercury	♅ Uranus	☋ South Node	▲ Super-Sensitivity
♊ Gemini	♍ Virgo	♒ Aquarius	♀ Venus	♆ Neptune	➡ Enters	▼ Low-Vitality
	♎ Libra	♓ Pisces	♂ Mars	♇ Pluto	℞ Retrograde	
	♏ Scorpio	☉ Sun	♃ Jupiter	⚷ Chiron	S/D Stationary Direct	

November

Sunday	Monday	Tuesday	Wednesday	Thursday	Friday	Saturday
						1 ♅♆⚷℞ All Saint's Day ☽→♓ 9:36AM 2. Choose not to go to extremes.
2 ♅♆⚷℞ PST begins 3. Let your experience create joy.	3 ♅♆⚷℞ ☽ V/C 1:05AM ☽→♈ 10:53AM 4. Dependability is a solid foundation.	4 ♅♆⚷℞ 5. With flexibility, change happens.	5 ♅♆⚷℞ ☽ V/C 5:24AM ☽→♉ 1:32PM 6. Plan a small dinner party.	6 ♅♆⚷℞ ○ 14°♉26′ 2:22PM 7. Read a book to stretch your mind.	7 ♅♆⚷℞ ☽ V/C 8:16AM ☽→♊ 5:44PM 8. Tolerance aids in being successful.	8 ♅♆⚷℞ ▼ ♀→♏ 3:10PM 9. Return to love.
9 ♅♆⚷℞ ▼ ☽ V/C 8:21AM 10. Use an innovative approach.	10 ♅♆⚷℞ ☽→♋ 12:37AM 2. A logical progression creates balance.	11 ♅♆⚷℞ Veteran's Day 3. Take time out for joy.	12 ♅♆⚷℞ ☽ V/C 1:16AM ☽→♌ 10:44AM 4. Notice the structure that works.	13 ♅♆⚷℞ 5. Spend some time in the sun.	14 ♅♆⚷℞ ☽ V/C 6:52PM ☽→♍ 11:08PM 6. Give some flowers just for fun.	15 ♅⚷℞ ♆SD-4°♓47′-11:07PM 7. Let your genius out.
16 ♅⚷℞ ♀→♐ 11:05AM 8. Enjoy the abundance in your life.	17 ♅⚷℞ ☽ V/C 3:11AM ☽→♎ 11:29AM 9. Be sure to follow your intuition.	18 ♅⚷℞ 10. There are many ways to reach a goal.	19 ♅⚷℞ ☽ V/C 6:24AM ☽→♏ 9:30PM 2. Stop vacillating. Make a decision.	20 ♅⚷℞ 3. Carry a song in your heart.	21 ♅⚷℞ ☽ V/C 9:53PM 4. Put all the pieces together logically.	22 ♅⚷℞ ● 0°♐07′ 4:32 AM ☽→♐ 4:19AM ☉→♐ 1:39AM 5. Make a productive change.
23 ♅℞ ▲ ☽ V/C 7:16PM ⚷SD-13°♓06′-3:43PM 6. An open heart is a trusting heart.	24 ♅℞ ▲ ☽→♑ 8:31AM 7. See all the reasons why an idea works.	25 ♅℞ 8. To succeed, be a good team member.	26 ♅℞ ☽ V/C 7:29AM ☽→♒ 11:22AM 9. The power of prayer is unlimited.	27 ♅℞ Thanksgiving Day ♀→♐ 6:27PM 10. Release all fear and move on.	28 ♅℞ ☽ V/C 9:14AM ☽→♓ 2:03PM 2. Emotional balance is healing.	29 ♅℞ 3. Use your imagination to have fun.
30 ♅℞ ☽ V/C 12:47PM ☽→♈ 5:13PM 4. Make a space that works for you.						

Full Moon in Taurus

November 6, 2:22 PM

Degree Choice Points
  14° Taurus 25'

Motivation Worldly

Resistance Weathering storms

Statement I Have
  Body Neck
  Mind Collector
  Spirit Accumulation

Element
  Earth – Self-value, abundant, collector, entrepreneurial, art, beauty, flowers, gardening, shopping, luxury, comfort, sensuousness.

Second House Moon
  1° Taurus 51'

Motivation Awe-inspiring

Resistance Dread

Second House Umbrella Theme
  I Have – The way you make your money and the way you spend your money to determine self-value.

Karmic Awakening

Become aware when you find your dreaming power and your manifesting power at a standstill. Storage of unleashed, raw power can become explosive and the manifesting moment becomes lost.

The Sun is Opposite the Moon

Full Moons are always in opposition to the Sun. This creates a feeling of tension between where you want to shine and how your feelings are flowing on a sensory level about the Sun's directive. The two forces seem like they are working against each other, yet they are on the same team displaying different techniques to attain the same goal. The Taurus/Scorpio polarity creates tension between shared resources and individual resources.

Taurus God

Ganesh is the Lord of Wisdom and Destroyer of All Obstacles. He grants success, prosperity, and protection against adversity. He is the deity that rules merchants and their trading. He rules Dharma by creating and removing obstacles appropriate to each individual's pathway. He is called the Lord of Wisdom because when we have earned the right to have an obstacle removed, we have learned the lesson and gained wisdom. Ganesh always appears with a rat at his feet. The rat is a symbol of desire, and desire always presents us with an obstacle to overcome in order to attain our wish. The rat shows up in secret places, stealing what does not belong to him. When the Moon is full in Taurus, it is time to put Ganesh into operation. Ask Ganesh to set us free from obstacles in order to gain wisdom and fulfill our desires.

On Your Altar

Colors Scarlet, earth tones

Numerology 7 – stretch your mind today

Tarot Card Hierophant – spiritual authority

Gemstones Red coral, red agate, garnet

Plant remedy Angelica – connecting Heaven and Earth

Fragrance Rose – opening the heart

Meditation

The freedom themes are provided by the zodiac sign and can be from this lifetime or other lifetimes. These meditations assist in dissolving blocks and opening pathways to new frontiers.

When the Moon is in Taurus, sit quietly, close your eyes, and breathe in and out. It is now time to search the Records of Stewardship to see where ownership of people and property may have been out of control. Look through the records to determine attitudes regarding possessions, objects of art, money, spending, lending, saving, and giving that may have been too extreme or impoverished. Ask for a Guardian Angel to show you where envy might be out of balance. Correct any dependency on others for their ability to acquire. Accept your own abundance factor.

Taurus Challenges and Victories

Say all of the statements in this section out loud. Then, underline the phrase that means the most to you. Use the phrase as your special affirmation for manifesting and co-creating throughout this phase of the moon.

Everything is possible for me today. My possibilities are endless. I have the power within me to make all of my dreams come true. I have the tools to make my talent a reality. I have the power to identify with my talent. Today, I focus my attention and intention on manifesting with my talent and, in so doing, I transform my ideas into reality. I recognize the part of me that is connected to the cosmic source of ideas and I express that source within me to manifest my creative power. I see my possibilities and act on them today. I am the creative power. I am all-knowing. I am an individual. There is no one else like me. I can manifest anything I desire. I intend it. I allow it. So be it.

Rules for Manifesting: know what you want, write it down, and say it out loud. Recognize that because you thought it, it can be so. Release your limiting beliefs. Override your limiting beliefs with power statements. Act as if you have already manifested your idea. Lastly, value yourself!

Taurus Homework

Newsflash for Taurus freedom process: consumerism is not practicing abundance. Take a look at what you have accumulated over the last few days, months, and years. Eliminate what no longer resonates to the beauty of the now. Take some of these items to a charity of your choice or give gifts to admiring friends. Take the Taurus freedom test and go to the store where you made your last purchase and return the items. Do not buy anything else. Remember, quality not quantity, and take the pledge to become a wise steward of your resources.

It's time to transform priorities from the external world of the centralized self, into the depth and subtlety of the hidden forces below the surface that connect us to the vastness of existence.

Full Moon in Taurus

November 6, 2:22 PM

Clearing the Slate for Freedom

Remember a time when you experienced the following trigger points. Write down what happened, forgive yourself, release it, and let it go to clear your slate for freedom.

Hoarding

- Forgive
- Release
- Let go

Stubborn

- Forgive
- Release
- Let go

Greedy

- Forgive
- Release
- Let go

Irresponsible Stewardship

- Forgive
- Release
- Let go

Wasteful

- Forgive
- Release
- Let go

My Freedom List

Taurus Freedom List Ideas

Now is the time to set myself free from envy, financial insecurity, being stubborn, hoarding, addictive spending, not feeling valuable, and fear of change.

Full Moon in Taurus

November 6, 2:22 PM

How to Use the Moon Book With Your Chart

Fill in the blanks on the Cosmic Check-In page. Then look up the degree of the moon on the chart below. Take note of the "I" statement on the outside of the wheel where the moon is located. Now locate the same degree on your own chart, and make a note of the house and corresponding "I" statement. Go back to the Cosmic Check-In page and circle the two statements from the charts and read what you wrote. This will give you an idea about what to expect from this moon phase on a personal level.

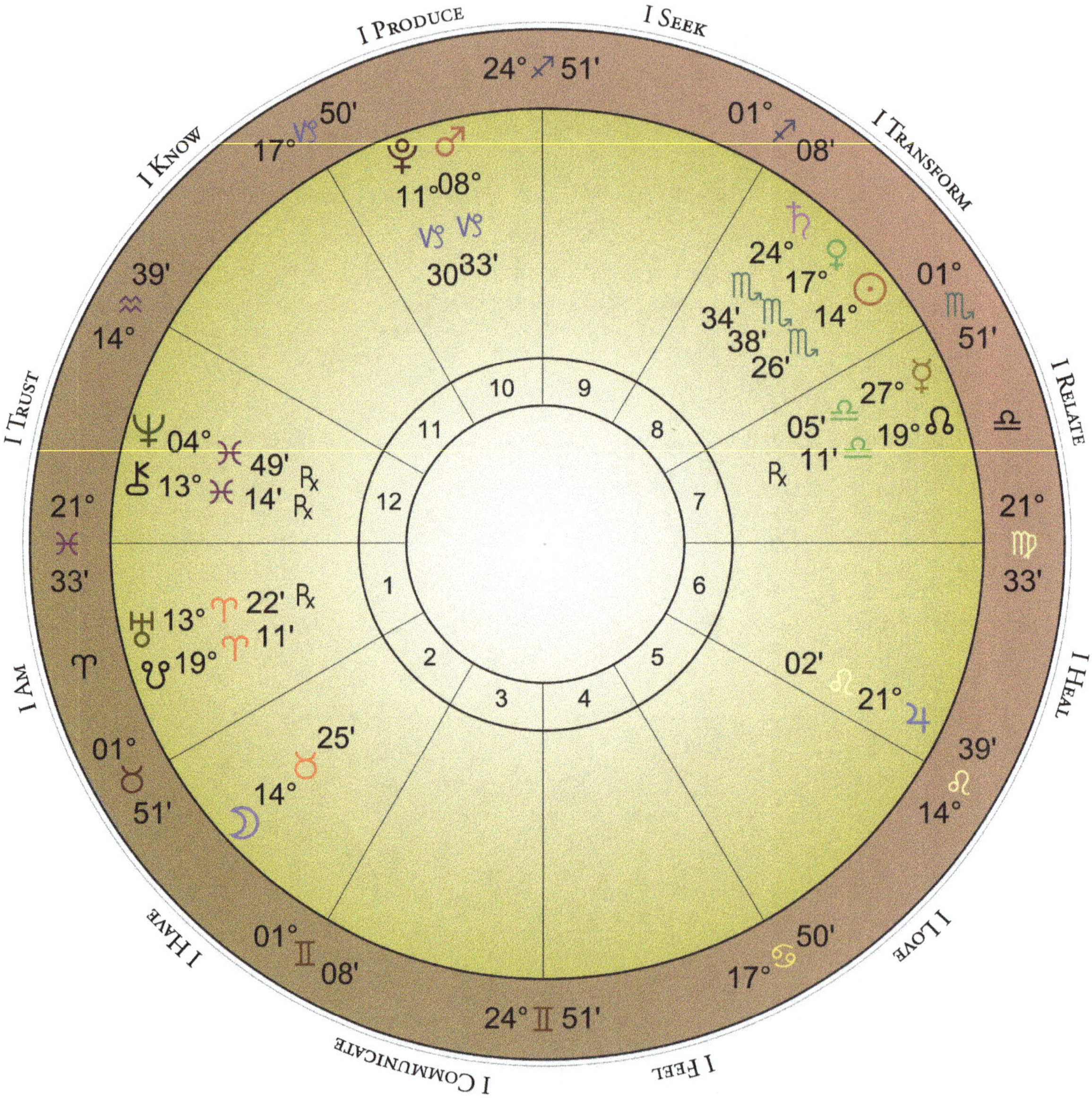

♈ Aries	♋ Cancer	♐ Sagittarius	☽ Moon	♄ Saturn	☊ North Node	V/C Void-of-Course
♉ Taurus	♌ Leo	♑ Capricorn	☿ Mercury	♅ Uranus	☋ South Node	▲ Super-Sensitivity
♊ Gemini	♍ Virgo	♒ Aquarius	♀ Venus	♆ Neptune	➡ Enters	▼ Low-Vitality
	♎ Libra	♓ Pisces	♂ Mars	♇ Pluto	℞ Retrograde	
	♏ Scorpio	☉ Sun	♃ Jupiter	⚷ Chiron	S/D Stationary Direct	

Cosmic Check-In

Take a moment to write a brief phrase for each "I" statement.
This activates all areas of your life for this creative cycle.

♉ I Have

♊ I Communicate

♋ I Feel

♌ I Love

♍ I Heal

♎ I Relate

♏ I Transform

♐ I Seek

♑ I Produce

♒ I Know

♓ I Trust

♈ I Am

MB7OXM3P5N4MB/LZDKFUGTO EH TI WHGS62 5 9 4H TAW KNGXBO E 2I3HEG

New Moon in Sagittarius

November 22, 4:32 AM

When the Sun is in Sagittarius

Now is the time for greater expansion of consciousness. Sagittarius is about exterminating all of the man-eating symbols of our illusions, harmful thoughts, inertia, prejudices, and superstitions that hide behind our excuses. It is truth time, so that the Soul Goal of the Sagittarius can come into being and direct its light toward greater aspiration. Questions to ask yourself at this time are: What is my goal for myself? What is my goal for my nation? What is my goal for humanity? All goals get stimulated during this time.

Sagittarius Goddess

The Sagittarius goddess, Saraswati, is in charge of fusing our personality with the light of our inner divinity. When this fusion occurs, the Law of Sound is made available to us and we have the power to manifest by directing our vision through the resonance of our own tone, note, or voice. The power of speech reaches a high level with Saraswati, the goddess of speech and knowledge. The activation of sound sheds light on our path, directing us toward the magnetic matrix of our future, our goals. Saraswati reminds us that everything we put to sound ultimately manifests. It is in our best interest to avoid harmful speech, gossip, and our story, in order to be present with the power of the moment. Call on Saraswati to deliver you to your point of experience that provides the knowledge you are here to gain.

On Your Altar

Colors Deep purple, deep blue, turquoise

Numerology 5 – prepare for change today

Tarot Card Temperance – blending physical and spiritual

Gemstones Turquoise, lapis

Plant Remedy Madia – seeing the target and hitting it

Fragrance Magnolia – expanded beauty

Degree Choice Points
0° Sagittarius 07'

Motivation Strengthening bonds

Resistance Coloring the past

Statement I Seek
  Body Thighs
  Mind Philosophical
  Spirit Inspiration

Element
Fire – Inspiring, leadership, charisma, igniting, adventure.

First House Moon
5° Scorpio 44'

Motivation Reliable enterprises

Resistance Opportunistic

First House Umbrella Theme
I Am – Your outer appearance, the way you present yourself, the way you dress, the way you enter a room, and what you leave behind when you leave the room.

My Co-Creation List

Sagittarius Co-Creation Ideas

Now is the time to focus on manifesting truth, teaching and study, understanding advanced ideas, optimism and inspiration, bliss, goals, travel and adventure, and philosophy and culture.

This, or something better than this, comes to me in an easy and pleasurable way for the good of all concerned. Thank you, Universe!

New Moon in Sagittarius

November 22, 4:32 AM

Sagittarius Challenges and Victories

Say all of the statements in this section out loud. Then, underline the phrase that means the most to you. Use the phrase as your special affirmation for manifesting and co-creating throughout this phase of the moon.

Destiny is in my favor today. I know, without a doubt, that I cannot make a wrong turn today. I access my blueprint to ensure perfect timing for all opportunities to be open to me today. I promise to be open to these opportunities, knowing full well that today is my day. I am on time and in time today. My destiny is here and working in my favor. I see all that is available to me today and claim my pathway to success. I pay attention to what comes my way today and know that it is an opening for good fortune to be my reality. I am ready to accept my good fortune now. All I have to do is move in the direction of my truth. I know that my truth is my good fortune. I trust in coincidence and synchronicity to provide me with direction to my destiny. All points of action lead me to my true expression. I can see clearly into my future today with great optimism. I intend it. I allow it. So be it. All is in Divine Order.

Mantra during this Time *(repeat this 10 times out loud)*

"My truth is my good fortune. My timing is perfect. I trust that all that comes to me today is in my highest and best good. I am open to optimism. The drum of destiny beats in my favor. So be it!"

Sagittarius Homework

Sagittarius co-creates best through teaching, publishing and writing, travel, spiritual adventures, and as tour group leaders, airline and cruise ship personnel, evangelical ministers, philosophers, anthropologists, linguists, and translators.

The Sagittarius moon cycle creates a magnetic matrix that stimulates us to take direction towards becoming one with a goal and then sheds light on the path. In the ancient mystery schools, Sagittarius moons were used to set the stage for candidates to reach higher levels of awareness by inspiring their desire to reach a goal and then to step toward the goal. It is time now to become one with my goal.

Without Acknowledgment Progress Cannot Occur

Acknowledgment creates space for victory and gratitude, which automatically brings us to a level of completion so a new cycle of opportunity can occur in our lives. When we celebrate our wins and acknowledge our victories with gratitude, we update our cells so that our ability to move forward is not hindered by a cellular holographic pattern that is stuck in the past. Cellular lag creates resistance and makes moving forward most difficult. The key is to stay continuously updated by acknowledging yourself for what you did do at the end of each day rather than heading off to sleep thinking about what you did not do. By acknowledging what we didn't do, we play into our karmic storage bank and keep our progress at bay. When we acknowledge ourselves and our manifestations, we are complete, and more cycles of opportunity become available to us in each new day. Be prepared for miracles.

Victory List

Gratitude List

This fulfills the relationship between the giver and the receiver, which completes the cycle with the Universe so that a new beginning can be established.

New Moon in Sagittarius

November 22, 4:32 AM

How to Use the Moon Book With Your Chart

Fill in the blanks on the Cosmic Check-In page. Then look up the degree of the moon on the chart below. Take note of the "I" statement on the outside of the wheel where the moon is located. Now locate the same degree on your own chart, and make a note of the house and corresponding "I" statement. Go back to the Cosmic Check-In page and circle the two statements from the charts and read what you wrote. This will give you an idea about what to expect from this moon phase on a personal level.

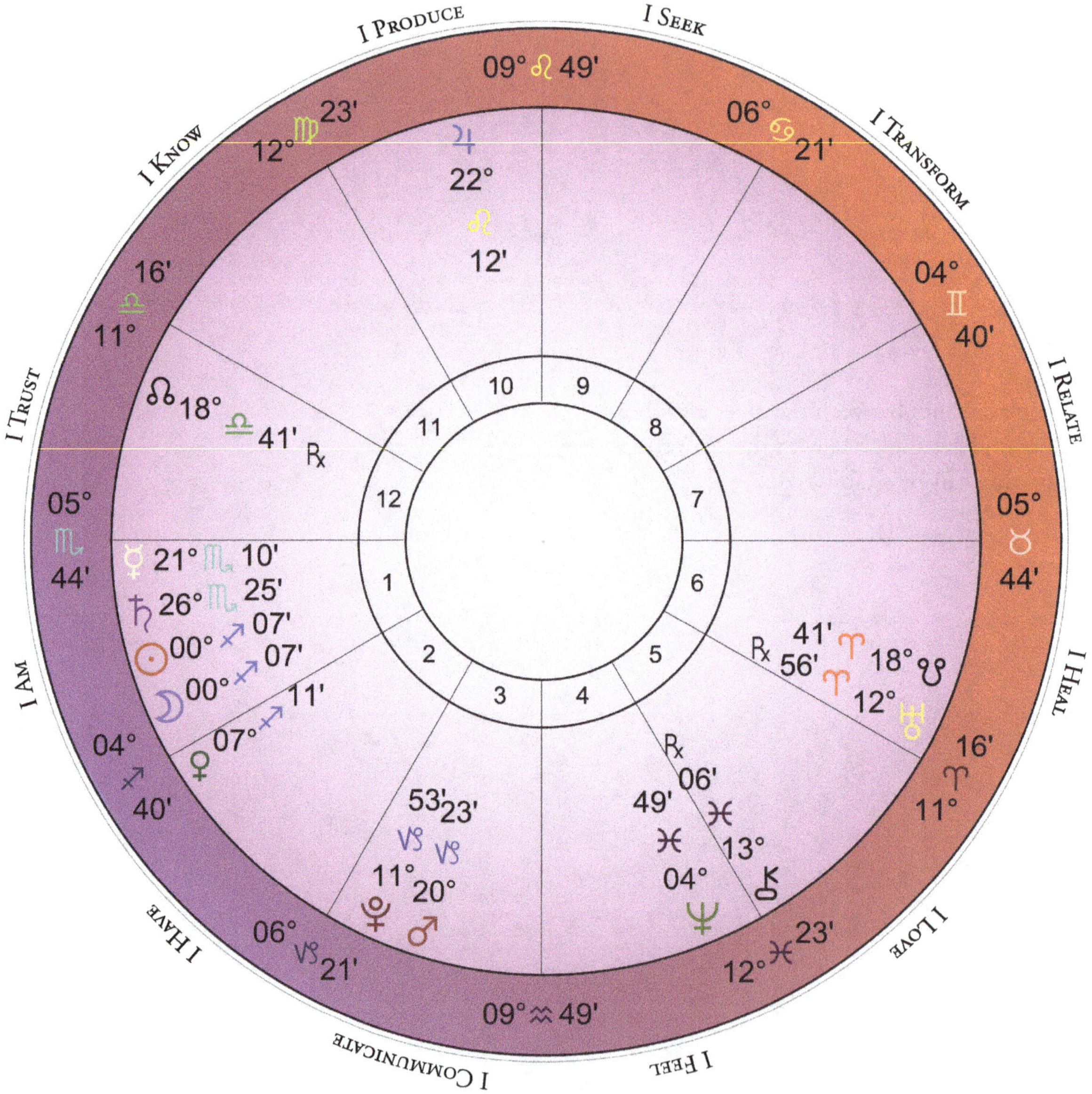

♈ Aries	♋ Cancer	♐ Sagittarius	☽ Moon	♄ Saturn	☊ North Node	V/C Void-of-Course
♉ Taurus	♌ Leo	♑ Capricorn	☿ Mercury	♅ Uranus	☋ South Node	▲ Super-Sensitivity
♊ Gemini	♍ Virgo	♒ Aquarius	♀ Venus	♆ Neptune	➡ Enters	▼ Low-Vitality
	♎ Libra	♓ Pisces	♂ Mars	♇ Pluto	℞ Retrograde	
	♏ Scorpio	☉ Sun	♃ Jupiter	⚷ Chiron	S/D Stationary Direct	

214

Cosmic Check-In

Take a moment to write a brief phrase for each "I" statement.
This activates all areas of your life for this creative cycle.

♐ I Seek

♑ I Produce

♒ I Know

♓ I Trust

♈ I Am

♉ I Have

♊ I Communicate

♋ I Feel

♌ I Love

♍ I Heal

♎ I Relate

♏ I Transform

December Planetary Highlights

Uranus Continues to be Retrograde in Aries until December 21

We are asked to complete all of our unfinished projects before the 21st, so that afterwards we can be free to move forward to new areas of endeavor with true enthusiasm. Do what it takes to cross the finish line on time so the true spirit of Uranus' theme "inner freedom" can be yours. Celebrate your completion with a ritual to open your cellular structure to receive your new magnetic matrix for the future. Prepare to become your future self!!!

December 6 – Jupiter goes Retrograde in Cancer

It's time to renew your faith in life. Notice where you have lost faith and see where you might want to recharge those areas by seeing positive outcomes. Check in with people that you haven't seen for a while and renew these relationships, where appropriate. If old friends contact you, be willing to check in to see what needs to be updated or released. 2002 is the year that needs to be updated now. Do a check in on that time, so that you can clean your slate before this year is over.

Expect family ties to come up and dominate your personal life, especially if you have a deep need to belong. Do a reality check on this belonging to see if you resonate with the idea that you belong to yourself first. Self-pity and past emotional issues, that are totally outdated, could stifle you and keep you from your future focus. Check in to see when you were controlled by your own fear of abandonment or rejection issues and allowed yourself to be hurt or manipulated because of your weakness in these areas.

December 4 – Mars Enters Aquarius

Mind expansion comes forward with some major ideas that can play a very important part in the areas of progress, evolution, and making the world a better place. Innovation goes to the top of the priority list right now.

December 10 – Venus Enters Capricorn

It's time to face the practical world and bring yourself back down to Earth. If you want to get into the mood for holiday shopping, do it before this date. If you want to watch your budget, shop after this date.

December 16 – Mercury Enters Capricorn

Misunderstanding is in the air, especially at work. There is a tendency here to sound too bossy. Defensive reactions could put you in a position to exhaust your mind.

December 21 – Winter Solstice – The Sun Enters Capricorn

It is the Earth's birthday! Celebrate the light of the new year with a candle celebration. Focus on what it will take for "success" to become your middle name.

December 23 – Saturn Enters Sagittarius

This is a game changer! We now leave the caverns of the deep parts of the mind and find the teacher standing in front of our faces asking us to point our noses to the doorway of truth. Honesty will be a key factor here, especially in the area of religion and spiritual studies. Foreign trade, education, and astronomy will all come up for re-discovery and enhancement.

Low-Vitality – December 5-7 ▼

This is a time when the Earth is low in energy. Pay particular attention to timing on these days. Stay on time and on purpose to manage your energy. If you find yourself out of sync in the timing zone, stop and start over again. Rushing leads to burn-out.

Super-Sensitivity – December 5-7, 9, 12-21 ▲

This is a time when the global atmosphere is sensitive. Watch out for obsessive thinking that can damage your self-esteem. Keep your ego from overloading your mind with judgments and devaluation.

♈ Aries	♋ Cancer	♐ Sagittarius	☽ Moon	♄ Saturn	☊ North Node	V/C Void-of-Course
♉ Taurus	♌ Leo	♑ Capricorn	☿ Mercury	♅ Uranus	☋ South Node	▲ Super-Sensitivity
♊ Gemini	♍ Virgo	♒ Aquarius	♀ Venus	♆ Neptune	➔ Enters	▼ Low-Vitality
	♎ Libra	♓ Pisces	♂ Mars	♇ Pluto	℞ Retrograde	
	♏ Scorpio	☉ Sun	♃ Jupiter	⚷ Chiron	S/D Stationary Direct	

December

Sunday	Monday	Tuesday	Wednesday	Thursday	Friday	Saturday
	1 ♅℞ 5. Make any change heart based.	2 ♅℞ ☽ V/C 6:41PM ☽→♉ 9:14PM 6. Keep your heart open by love.	3 ♅℞ 7. Study to attain trust, not control.	4 ♅℞ ☽ V/C 10:44PM ♂→♒ 3:58PM 8. Manifest what you love.	5 ♅℞ ▲ ☽→♊ 2:28AM 9. Strive for spiritual clarity.	6 ♅℞ ▼ ▲ ○14°♊18′ 4:26AM 10. Choose new beginnings wisely.
7 ♅℞ ▼ ▲ ☽ V/C 1:51AM ☽→♋ 9:34AM 11. Feel equal with others.	8 ♃♅℞ ▲ ♃℞-22°♌37′ 12:42PM 3. A playful attitude opens doors easily.	9 ♃♅℞ ▲ ☽ V/C 4:14PM ☽→♌ 7:14PM 4. Trust the framework you create.	10 ♃♅℞ ♀→♑ 8:43AM 5. Be a part of the change.	11 ♃♅℞ 6. An open heart heals relationships.	12 ♃♅℞ ▲ ☽ V/C 4:48AM ☽→♍ 7:18AM 7. Learn from what others teach.	13 ♃♅℞ ▲ 8. Enjoy material goods.
14 ♃♅℞ ▲ ☽ V/C 6:10PM ☽→♎ 8:04PM 9. Spiritual clarity comes with prayer.	15 ♃♅℞ ▲ 10. Release the past to begin anew.	16 ♃♅℞ ▲ Chanukah ☽ V/C 9:39PM ☿→♑ 7:54PM 11. Know the universe is unlimited.	17 ♃♅℞ ▲ ☽→♏ 6:51AM 3. Allow experience to become belief.	18 ♃♅℞ ▲ 4. A building is as good as it's base.	19 ♃♅℞ ▲ ☽ V/C 1:11PM ☽→♐ 1:55PM 5. When in doubt, change.	20 ♃♅℞ ▲ 6. Action deepens a relationship.
21 ♃℞ ▲ ●0°♑06′ 5:35PM ☽ V/C 4:34AM ☽→♑ 5:24PM Winter Solstice ☉→♑ 3:04PM ♅D-12°♈34′ 2:46PM 7. Make learning a joy in your life.	22 ♃℞ ☽ V/C 7:16PM 8. Meet your needs first, then others.	23 ♃℞ ☽→♒ 6:52PM ♄→♐ 8:34AM 9. Refresh with the music of the season.	24 ♃℞ 10. Look forward to a happy beginning.	25 ♃℞ Christmas Day ☽ V/C 7:10AM ☽→♓ 8:06PM 11. Make this a day for true celebration.	26 ♃℞ 3. Make today a play day for you.	27 ♃℞ ☽ V/C 7:43AM ☽→♈ 10:35PM 4. Plan a celebration that feels good.
28 ♃℞ 5. Allow your travel plans to be playful.	29 ♃℞ ☽ V/C 4:45PM 6. Spend special time with your love.	30 ♃℞ ☽→♉ 2:55AM 7. Learn something about the new year.	31 ♃℞ New Year's Eve 8. Give thanks for all the year gave us.			

Full Moon in Gemini

December 6, 4:26 AM

Degree Choice Points
 14° Gemini 17'

Motivation Like-mindedness

Resistance Seduction

Statement I Communicate
  Body Lungs
  Mind Duplicity
  Spirit Communication

Element
 Air – Promotes curiosity, insight, concepts, and brings change.

Seventh House Moon
 15° Taurus 58'

Motivation Tenacity

Resistance Backstory

Seventh House Umbrella Theme
 I Relate – One-on-one relationships, defines your people attraction, and how you work in relationships with the people you attract.

The Sun is Opposite the Moon

Full Moons are always in opposition to the Sun. This creates a feeling of tension between where you want to shine and how your feelings are flowing on a sensory level about the Sun's directive. The two forces seem like they are working against each other, yet they are on the same team displaying different techniques to attain the same goal. The Gemini/Sagittarius polarity creates tension between community ideas and global thinking.

Gemini Goddess

Echo means, "one who loves her own voice." Echo was a very talkative nymph who lived in the garden of Bacchus. Zeus visited this garden often to survey the desirable nymphs. He was enchanted by the gregarious Echo and began his conquest for her. Hera, Zeus' wife, arrived just as he was about to consummate his passion for Echo. Hera was so jealous that she punished the talkative Echo for flirting with her husband. She took away Echo's ability to converse, leaving her to repeat the last three words of other people's sentences. When the Moon is full in Gemini, it is time to look at our mindless chatter and release repeating thoughts that echo in the chamber of our mind.

On Your Altar

Colors Bright yellow, orange, multi-colors

Numerology 10 – set the stage for something new!

Tarot Card Lovers – connecting to wholeness

Gemstones Yellow diamond, citrine, yellow jade, yellow topaz

Plant remedy Morning Glory – thinking with your heart, not your head

Fragrance Iris – the ability to focus the mind

Meditation

The freedom themes are provided by the zodiac sign and can be from this lifetime or other lifetimes. These meditations assist in dissolving blocks and opening pathways to new frontiers.

When the Moon is in Gemini, it is a time to review the split between your spiritual nature and your worldly nature. Sit down and close your eyes. Breathe in and breathe out. Ask for the Angel of Blending to bring you awareness of your double-mindedness, double-speaking, criticism of others, discontent, and mental unrest. Become aware of separation issues that divide you from your personal truth and be a unifier, rather than a divider.

Gemini Challenges and Victories

Say all of the statements in this section out loud. Then, underline the phrase that means the most to you. Use the phrase as your special affirmation for manifesting and co-creating throughout this phase of the moon.

Today, I blend my old self with my new self, my physical reality with my spiritual awareness, my positive thoughts with my negative thoughts, my past with my present, my feminine with my masculine, my rewards with my losses, my ups with my downs, and my higher self with my lower self. It is a day for me to refine and fine tune my life by looking at my extremes. I recognize what inspires me and what keeps me stuck. I find my center today by acknowledging my extremes. I am aware that balance comes to those who are able to locate the space in the center of these opposite energy fields.

When I am in my center, my polarities are in motion. Healing cannot occur unless my polarities are moving and I know that healing is motion. I am ready for a healing today. I know that by visiting my opposites, and determining their vast opposition to each other, I can find the paradoxes that I have chosen for myself and begin to heal. I am willing to experiment with this blending of opposites and become the alchemist of my own life. When I blend all aspects of myself, rather than separating them, I can truly become whole. Today is a day to integrate, rather than separate, in order to release the spark of light that stays a prisoner when my polarities are in operation. When I find balance, motion occurs and the Law of Harmony takes over, putting paradoxical energies to rest, thus breaking the crystallization of polarity. The Law of Harmony is beauty in motion and promotes the flow of color, light, sound, and movement into form. Balance is a condition that keeps my spark in motion. I become the vertical line in the center of polarity today and carry the secret of balance. Balance cannot be my goal, motion is my goal today. When I am in motion, I can take action to evolve and to express all of myself freely.

Gemini Homework

Sit still and invite silence into your space. Stay quiet and still for at least 5 minutes. During this time take an inventory and see where you have interrupted people in the middle of their sentences. Now is the time to make a conscious effort to allow others the space to express their thoughts. Keep sitting there in silence and feel the frustration, while embracing the power of silence.

Full Moon in Gemini

December 6, 4:26 AM

Clearing the Slate for Freedom

Remember a time when you experienced the following trigger points. Write down what happened, forgive yourself, release it, and let it go to clear your slate for freedom.

Gossiping

- Forgive
- Release
- Let go

Omitting the Truth

- Forgive
- Release
- Let go

Not Listening / Talking Too Much

- Forgive
- Release
- Let go

Hyperactivity

- Forgive
- Release
- Let go

Sales Manipulation and Marketing

- Forgive
- Release
- Let go

My Freedom List

Gemini Freedom List Ideas

Now is the time to set myself free from unfinished business, shallow communication, old files and office clutter, lies I tell myself, broken communication devices, temptation to gossip, restlessness, over-thinking, and vacillation.

Full Moon in Gemini

December 6, 4:26 AM

How to Use the Moon Book With Your Chart

Fill in the blanks on the Cosmic Check-In page. Then look up the degree of the moon on the chart below. Take note of the "I" statement on the outside of the wheel where the moon is located. Now locate the same degree on your own chart, and make a note of the house and corresponding "I" statement. Go back to the Cosmic Check-In page and circle the two statements from the charts and read what you wrote. This will give you an idea about what to expect from this moon phase on a personal level.

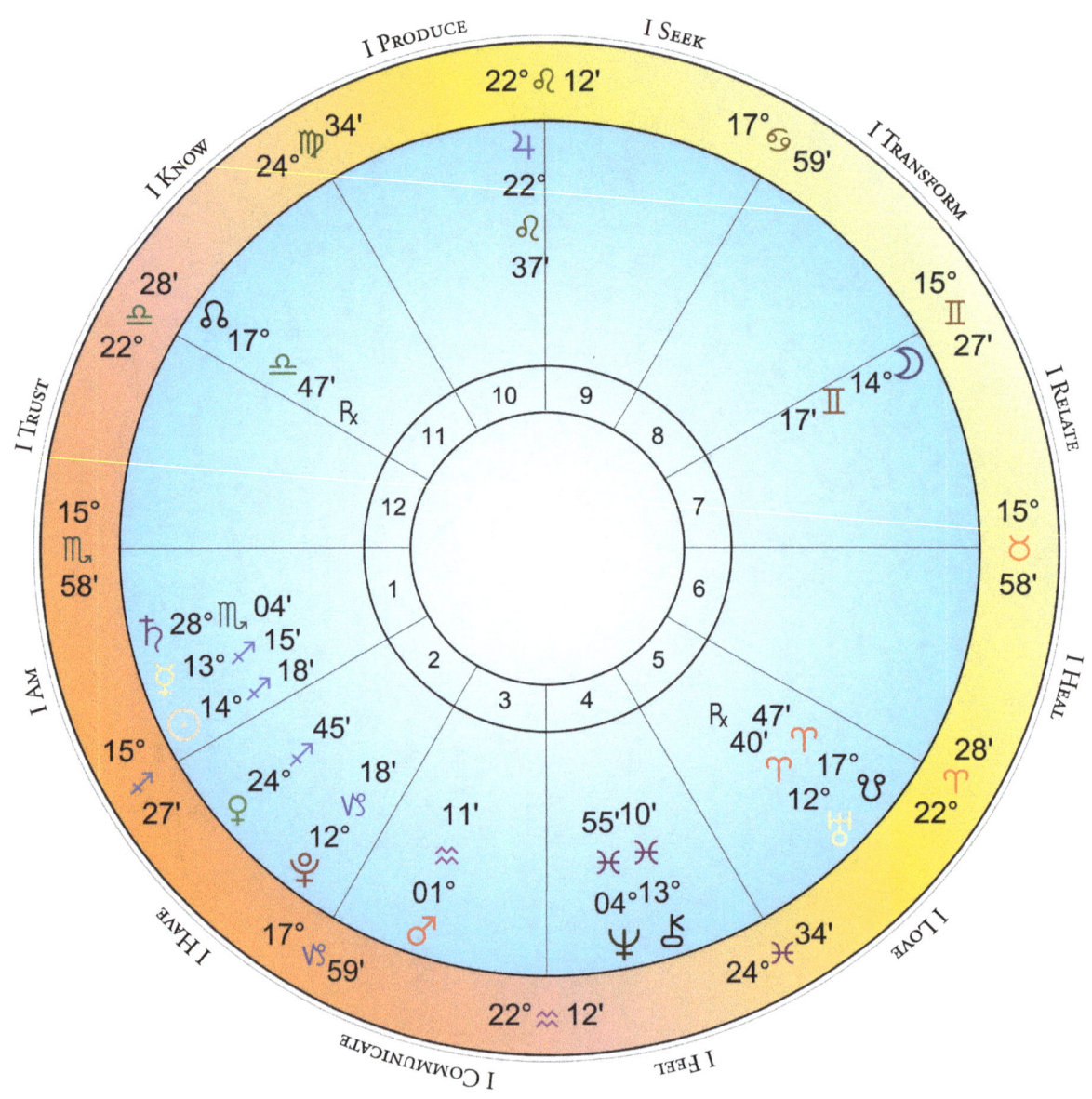

♈ Aries	♋ Cancer	♐ Sagittarius	☽ Moon	♄ Saturn	☊ North Node	V/C Void-of-Course
♉ Taurus	♌ Leo	♑ Capricorn	☿ Mercury	♅ Uranus	☋ South Node	▲ Super-Sensitivity
♊ Gemini	♍ Virgo	♒ Aquarius	♀ Venus	♆ Neptune	➡ Enters	▼ Low-Vitality
	♎ Libra	♓ Pisces	♂ Mars	♇ Pluto	℞ Retrograde	
	♏ Scorpio	☉ Sun	♃ Jupiter	⚷ Chiron	S/D Stationary Direct	

224

Cosmic Check-In

Take a moment to write a brief phrase for each "I" statement.
This activates all areas of your life for this creative cycle.

♊ I Communicate

♋ I Feel

♌ I Love

♍ I Heal

♎ I Relate

♏ I Transform

♐ I Seek

♑ I Produce

♒ I Know

♓ I Trust

♈ I Am

♉ I Have

New Moon in Capricorn

December 21, 5:35 PM

Degree Choice Points
    0° Capricorn 06'

Motivation Worthy

Resistance Servility

Statement I Produce
    Body Knees
    Mind Authority issues
    Spirit Advance civilization

Element
    Earth – Security, patience, endurance, determination, unveiling your truth.

Sixth House Moon
    8° Sagittarius 45'

Motivation Step-by-step guidance

Resistance Hasty reactions

Sixth House Umbrella Theme
    I Heal – The way you manage your body and its appearance, habitual patterns, and the way you work.

When the Sun is in Capricorn

The statement for Capricorn is I Produce. It is important for all of us to feel useful and productive during this time. When the Sun is in this sign, we are given opportunities to receive the blessings of abundance and prosperity on a concrete level. Material satisfaction is at the top of the priority list for Capricorns. This is why they are known to be ambitious. Let integrity and goodwill set the standard for your recognition and accomplishments. Now is the time to take advantage of the energy by being useful and productive with a higher purpose. Capricorn is going through the most difficult times right now as the old guard is being swept away and creating space for the opening of the human heart. The presence of Pluto in this constellation is transforming all the systems and structures that are so familiar and placing Capricorn on unstable ground. Authority symbols and traditions are dissolving and opening new pathways for self-reliance to emerge as a reality, so that the idea of elitism can diminish and synergy will be the new status quo.

Capricorn God

Khronos is the god of time. He is an incorporeal god who emerged formless at the beginning of Creation. In the beginning, he demonstrated this by creating himself as a snake with three heads: one a man, one a bull, and one a lion, all symbols of the primal world. Khronos is the consort to Anake, the goddess of inevitability. Together they circle the primal world weaving a tapestry of spirals that connect the Earth directly to the Ordered Universe, so that time can be birthed and everything will have an order to it. When the Moon is full in Capricorn, we must become free of our concern about time and learn to trust in the concept of inevitability by calling on the power of Khronos and Anake to know about timing.

On Your Altar

Colors Forest green, tan, earth tones, deep red

Numerology 7 – learn something new!

Tarot Card The Devil – being a prisoner of a choice-less reality

Gemstones Topaz, carnelian, amber, smoky quartz, jasper

Plant Remedy Rosemary – the power of memory

Fragrance Frankincense – opens the gateway for the Soul to enter the body

My Co-Creation List

Capricorn
Co-Creation Ideas

Now is the time to focus on manifesting flexibility, productivity, authenticity, timing, new paradigms, transmuting, transformation, and re-translating structure.

This, or something better than this, comes to me in an easy and pleasurable way for the good of all concerned. Thank you, Universe!

New Moon in Capricorn

December 21, 5:35 PM

Capricorn Challenges and Victories

Say all of the statements in this section out loud. Then, underline the phrase that means the most to you. Use the phrase as your special affirmation for manifesting and co-creating throughout this phase of the moon.

Ultimate fulfillment is mine today! My willingness to live my life to the fullest each day is making all my dreams come true. I am fulfilling the promise of my destiny, and, in so doing, I make my mark on the world. I have completed my commitment to the Earth and to the cosmos by being all that I can be in the cycles of time on the inner and outer planes of awareness. All four seasons have been activated within me so that I am in alignment and in motion with the cycles of releasing, rebirthing, planting and harvesting.

I can now claim my citizenship in all four worlds. I am open and ready for the inspiration that the spirit world brings me. I am ready to conquer the mental world by using thought rather than thinking. I am open to the expression of my heart and the magnetic field of love that is ever-present in my experience. I am open to receiving abundance from Nature and I contribute to the physical world by actively manifesting my ideas into reality.

I am in harmony with the four elements and keep them active within me, as well as contribute to them externally. The element of air is within me as I breathe in the miracle of life. The element of earth is within me as I honor my body and use all its senses to enhance the quality of life. I honor the earth as my home and take complete stewardship of my home and property on this earth. I honor the water, the wellspring of life eternal, and allow for the flow of my feelings and emotions to be a creative influence in the unconscious and conscious planes. I honor the fire within me as the spark of light that is a source of inspiration in my experience, and in so doing I have fulfilled the promise of my destiny to live fully, freely, and passionately on all levels and on all dimensions with my Earth-Cosmos connection.

Capricorn Homework

The Capricorn Moon is the reincarnation of Spirit emerging from the dark waters of our past emotions and releasing us from our fear of change and our fear of loss. Awaken your powerful and positive spiritual connection to be open to new possibilities. Ask yourself to move beyond your emotional loyalty to the past in order to co-create. We are reminded of our need for material and emotional security at this time. In order to insure this, we must learn to build a foundation for ourselves that is lit from within, made from the materials of love, goodwill, and intelligence. Give yourself permission to throw away your watch and celebrate living in the moment.

Without Acknowledgment Progress Cannot Occur

Acknowledgment creates space for victory and gratitude, which automatically brings us to a level of completion so a new cycle of opportunity can occur in our lives. When we celebrate our wins and acknowledge our victories with gratitude, we update our cells so that our ability to move forward is not hindered by a cellular holographic pattern that is stuck in the past. Cellular lag creates resistance and makes moving forward most difficult. The key is to stay continuously updated by acknowledging yourself for what you did do at the end of each day rather than heading off to sleep thinking about what you did not do. By acknowledging what we didn't do, we play into our karmic storage bank and keep our progress at bay. When we acknowledge ourselves and our manifestations, we are complete, and more cycles of opportunity become available to us in each new day. Be prepared for miracles.

Victory List

Gratitude List

This fulfills the relationship between the giver and the receiver, which completes the cycle with the Universe so that a new beginning can be established.

New Moon in Capricorn

December 21, 5:35 PM

How to Use the Moon Book With Your Chart

Fill in the blanks on the Cosmic Check-In page. Then look up the degree of the moon on the chart below. Take note of the "I" statement on the outside of the wheel where the moon is located. Now locate the same degree on your own chart, and make a note of the house and corresponding "I" statement. Go back to the Cosmic Check-In page and circle the two statements from the charts and read what you wrote. This will give you an idea about what to expect from this moon phase on a personal level.

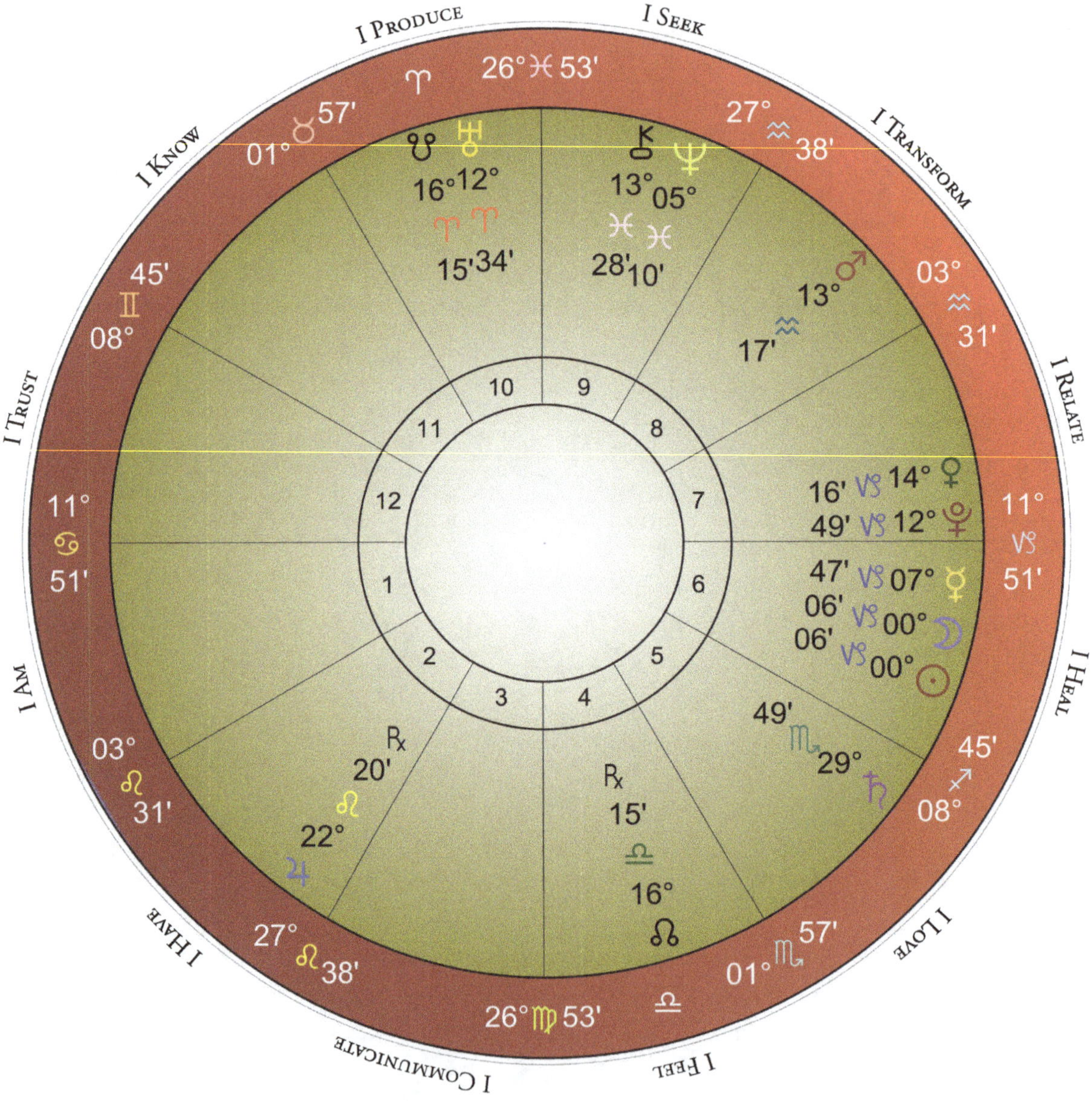

♈ Aries	♋ Cancer	♐ Sagittarius	☽ Moon	♄ Saturn	☊ North Node	V/C Void-of-Course
♉ Taurus	♌ Leo	♑ Capricorn	☿ Mercury	♅ Uranus	☋ South Node	▲ Super-Sensitivity
♊ Gemini	♍ Virgo	♒ Aquarius	♀ Venus	♆ Neptune	➡ Enters	▼ Low-Vitality
	♎ Libra	♓ Pisces	♂ Mars	♇ Pluto	℞ Retrograde	
	♏ Scorpio	☉ Sun	♃ Jupiter	⚷ Chiron	S/D Stationary Direct	

Cosmic Check-In

Take a moment to write a brief phrase for each "I" statement.
This activates all areas of your life for this creative cycle.

♑ I Produce

♒ I Know

♓ I Trust

♈ I Am

♉ I Have

♊ I Communicate

♋ I Feel

♌ I Love

♍ I Heal

♎ I Relate

♏ I Transform

♐ I Seek

About the Author

Beatrex Quntanna
is a dynamic teacher devoted to the growth and development of the human potential. She inspires, motivates, and stimulates growth with her ever-present zest for life and the human experience. Beatrex is an author, lecturer, symbolist, and tarot expert. She has been counseling and teaching for the past thirty years using the Tarot as an enhancement for personal and intuitive development. Her students find her workshops and books inspiring, enlightening, full of wise truths, and helpful in pursuing the most positive outcome in their own lives.

Beatrex is also the author of *Tarot: A Universal Language*, an easy-to-use approach to understanding the symbolism of tarot and applying it to daily life.

Interested in personal readings with Beatrex, and ongoing Moon Classes and workshops? Contact her at beatrex@cox.net or visit her at www.beatrex.com

Visit www.mymoonbook.com for Moon-related products created by Beatrex.

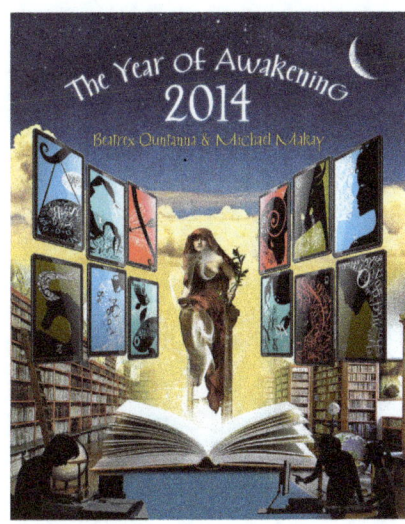

2014
The Year of Awakening Wall Calendar

By Beatrex Quntanna and Michael Makay

Astrological Calculations by Katherine Sale

This calendar is designed as a complete support system to enhance our understanding of how to best work with the planetary movements and numerological influences of the coming year.

It offers many tools and modalities to guide us through the entire year including…

- Astrological Highlights
- Daily Intentions based on Tibetan numerology
- Planetary Retrogrades listed monthly
- New Moons and Full Moons, referred to by time, astrological sign and degree
- Super-Sensitivity Days and Low-Vitality Days
- When the Sun enters a new Zodiac Sign

2014 is guaranteed to be a momentous year, especially for the Feminine, as we learn to awaken to the idea that changing paradigms are a reality and accept the idea that releasing the old guard is a blessing to our world and to our Earth. 2014 is all about moving the mind beyond thinking and transforming our thoughts into knowing. Knowing is the higher octave of the mind and asks us to "know and go." Knowing opens the doorway to our heart-mind becoming a reality…then, we can Live Love Every Day!

To order, call 1-760-944-6020
or go to www.mymoonbook.com

Tarot
A Universal Language

By Beatrex Quntanna

Experiencing The Road of Life
Through the Magic of Symbols

The symbology of each Major and Minor card are an awakening to the inner-wisdom of the Tarot—each card comes alive to a new light with upbeat, positive definitions that reflect Beatrex' fresh approach to life and living, making self-discovery easy and fun!

- Easy to use and easy to understand

- Includes an interpretation of all 78 Tarot cards right-side-up and reversed, in full-color

- Filled with innovative and informative readings for the reader to dive deep into the pool of knowledge and discover how to live vibrantly

Enthusiastic readers call it,

"Brilliantly Engineered"

"Amazingly Accurate"

"A refreshing, uncluttered approach to learning the Tarot."

**To order, call 1-760-944-6020
or go to www.Beatrex.com**

www.ingramcontent.com/pod-product-compliance
Lightning Source LLC
Chambersburg PA
CBHW080730230426
43665CB00020B/2685